No Greater Life

Embracing God's design for wholehearted love

Martin J. Young

malcolm down
PUBLISHING

First published 2026 by Malcolm Down Publishing Ltd.
www.malcolmdown.co.uk

28 27 26 6 5 4 3 2 1

British Library Cataloguing in Publication Data
A catalogue record for this book is available from the British Library.

ISBN 978-1-917455-51-0

Cover design by Mark Steel
Art direction by Sarah Grace

Printed in the UK

Typeset in the Grace Typeface

The Grace Typeface has been developed over many years in partnership with Sarah Grace, 2K Denmark and Cambridge University. This ground-breaking typeface aims to improve readability and reduce visual stress for people with dyslexia and other reading difficulties.

Contents

PART FOUR: Out To The World

Looking out: to love Jesus and our neighbours in our mission

PART FIVE: On The Road

Loving and listening as we choose to follow Jesus wherever he goes

Foreword

Every great story invites a response. Once we begin to see the vastness of God's story, his love that shaped creation, redeemed humanity, and still calls us today, we cannot remain spectators.

No Greater Life is about that response: what it means to live, breathe, and act in light of the story of a God who is beyond comparison.

If *No Greater Story* opened our eyes to the sweep of God's purposes, this next stage asks a deeper question: How do I live within that story? How does the knowledge of such love reshape my choices, renew my heart, and reorientate my daily life? The answer lies in the great commandment Jesus gave, 'to love the Lord your God with all your heart . . . soul . . . strength and . . . mind' (Luke 10:27). This is not a narrow rule, but an invitation to wholeness. To a life where every part of us is drawn into love.

Living this way is not about perfection but participation. It's about allowing God's story to reach into the ordinary corners of our lives, the commute, the kitchen table, the conversations we didn't plan. When we see life through the lens of God's love, even the smallest actions take on purpose. The way we speak, give, forgive and serve reflects the greater story unfolding through us.

I once met a guy who told me that his faith finally came alive not in a sermon or a study, but when he began quietly visiting an elderly neighbour each week. 'It was the first time I felt I was living God's story, not just hearing it,' he said. That is what this book is about. The Great Commandment isn't just theology, it's transformation. It calls us to live in a way that makes love visible, tangible and contagious.

As you move through these pages, you'll find ideas, reflections and practical ways to live out this wholehearted love. Let them challenge and stretch you. Allow them to draw you into the places where faith meets daily life.

I want to encourage you not just to read the words; let them lead you into action. Join in the activities, take the challenges to heart, and discover that there truly is no greater life than one lived fully in God's story.

Rev Dr Cris Rogers

Chair of Spring Harvest Planning Group and member of Board of Directors of Essential Christian

Introduction

This is a book about living and loving like Jesus. It is about finding out what kind of life Jesus lived and then imitating that. It is about being a disciple.

There are all kinds of ways we can describe discipleship. Discipleship is about following Jesus – walking in his footsteps, following in his way, being on a pilgrim journey. It is about learning – being an apprentice by practising the skills and habits of Jesus' way of life, obeying his commands and growing in knowledge and character. It is about imitation – doing what Jesus did, being his representative, spokesperson and ambassador. All these ways of understanding what a disciple is are essential and biblical and will be covered in this book.

The lens we will look through, nevertheless, will be the lens of love. Being a disciple is being someone who loves Jesus, and because of that they will live in such a way that Jesus is honoured, praised and pointed towards: 'And this is love: that we walk in obedience to his commands. As you have heard from the beginning, his command is that you walk in love' (2 John 1:6).

If we love Jesus, we will take up our cross and follow him (Matthew 10:37-39).

If we love Jesus, we will obey his commands (John 15:12-15).

If we love Jesus, we will mature and grow into being his body here on earth (Ephesians 4:15).

So, love encompasses all the teaching about being a disciple that comes from Jesus and the other apostles. It is not love that is shallow and flattering, or only ever softly accommodating. But it is certainly love that overcomes control, insecurity and religious duty, all of which can end up turning joyful and authentic discipleship into a rule-based system of earning our way to holiness. The sixteenth-century Carmelite sister, Teresa of Avila, in chapter four of her book about prayer and devotion, *Interior Castle*, famously writes:

> . . . the important thing is not to think much, but to love much; do, then, whatever most arouses you to love. Perhaps we do not know what love is: it would not surprise me a great deal to learn this, for love consists, not in the extent of our happiness, but in the firmness of our determination to try to please God in everything . . .[1]

This is how Jesus lived and loved – to glorify the Father, by bringing salvation and reconciliation to the world by proclaiming the good news of the kingdom of heaven – and it is how he calls us to live and love. So, the greatest commandment that he highlights from the whole of the Hebrew Bible is this: "'Love the Lord your God with all your heart and with all your soul and with all your mind and with all your strength.' The second is this: 'Love your neighbour as yourself'" (Mark 12:30-31). And when we do this, we inevitably desire to do the will of God: to follow in Jesus' footsteps; to live well and in a holy way, and to join in with Jesus' mission. If being a disciple of Jesus is all about love, then the place this love flows from is our heart. So whatever knowledge we learn, skills we acquire, habits we keep and experience we gain, it all comes from a newly born heart. Wholehearted Love is the Way.

1. Teresa of Avila, *Interior Castle* (Mineola, NY: Dover Publications, Inc., 2008).

Greater: A series of three books

This book is the middle of a series of three: *No Greater Story*; *No Greater Life*; *No Greater Adventure*. The first, written by Leon Evans,[2] was an overview of the Creative, Redemptive and Perfecting plan of God through history. It took us through the whole story of God from the very beginning and explored the book of Isaiah to reflect on God's plan for humanity, his plan for salvation and his plan for eternity. The third book, written by Sammy Jabangwe Hanton and Cris Rogers, will be all about the Great Commission. The sending of Jesus for us to receive the Holy Spirit and be his 'witnesses in Jerusalem . . . Judea . . . Samaria, and to the ends of the earth' (Acts 1:8). Its focus will be the book of Acts and how we can learn from the apostles how to live out this mission.

This book, then, is split into five parts, which are all about how to live no greater life than one that is wholehearted.

WHOLEHEARTED – No Greater Life than following the Greatest Commandment – how to live life to the full in God's world, God's way;

UP THE MOUNTAIN – Looking up: to love Jesus in our worship;

IN THE HOUSE – Looking in: to love Jesus and one another in Christ-centred communities;

OUT TO THE WORLD – Looking out: to love Jesus and our neighbours in our mission;

ON THE ROAD – Loving and listening as we choose to follow Jesus wherever he goes.

2. Leon Evans, *No Greater Story* (Welwyn Garden City: Malcolm Down Publishing, 2025).

How to read the book

Each chapter is split into three sections: Classroom, Living Room, Playground.

Classroom is an exploration of what the Bible says about each chapter's subject. Because we are highlighting the Greatest Commandment from Mark 12, this exploration will focus on Mark's account of how the disciples and others followed Jesus and how he taught and trained them. Jesus is mainly quoting from the book of Deuteronomy when he declares this great way of living, so this section will also focus on the teaching of Moses and the discipleship life of Israel as they prepare to live in the Promised Land.

Living Room is all about how we understand and learn from these teachings and examples in our lives today. It is application – how do we put into practice what the people of Israel were doing or what Jesus asked of his followers? What does that look like today in our own lives and communities? This will include holy habits and spiritual disciplines as well as examples from churches and ministries.

Playground is a kind of personal toolkit and small-group manual for reflecting, journalling, worshipping, exploring the Bible and engaging in spiritual habits. It is a collection of exercises, studies, prayers and resources – all practical ways of applying God's radical design to our everyday living. Each Playground session includes a Bible study that compares both struggling and transformational examples of discipleship in Mark's Gospel, as well as a study series on the heart. Every Playground session also includes a Lectio 365 exercise, from Carla Harding at 24-7 Prayer, covering the theme of each chapter. Lectio 365 Prayer is an app that facilitates guided prayer, Bible reading and reflection each day. It is inspired by the ancient practice of Lectio Divina (which means 'Divine

Reading'), a way of meditating on the Bible that's been used by Christians for centuries.

Pause, breathe deeply, and be still in God's presence
Rejoice with a psalm and reflect on Scripture
Ask God to help you and those you care about
Yield to God; welcome his love, his plans and his presence into your day.

Learning from one another

This will be a sentence or paragraph from a friend of Spring Harvest – a speaker, volunteer, artist or representative from a partner organisation.[3] They give their own tips and illustrations on discipleship, how they follow Jesus and what this means for them. (And don't forget their top tips for discipleship right at the end!) Scan the QR code at the end of each 'Playground' section to find further details on their ministry, church or resource. Here is an example:

> Being a disciple is to include Jesus in all our thoughts, decisions, actions; to live out his teachings with consistency, faithfulness and joy; to love, live and give of ourselves in every situation to the glory of God.
>
> (Simon Guillebaud, Speaker and Author, Great Lakes Outreach, Burundi)

The final part of this introduction will be a brief overview of Mark's Gospel and Deuteronomy, but before that, it may be a good idea to reflect and pray by meditating on some beautiful words of Jesus about what it means to be a disciple.

3. Edited for the purposes of this book.

This is how Jesus describes how to embrace God's design for a wholehearted life – glory, fruitfulness, keeping commands, joy, sacrifice, friendship, learning, prayer and of course, love.

> If you remain in me and my words remain in you, ask whatever you wish, and it will be done for you. This is to my Father's glory, that you bear much fruit, showing yourselves to be my disciples. As the Father has loved me, so have I loved you. Now remain in my love. If you keep my commands, you will remain in my love, just as I have kept my Father's commands and remain in his love. I have told you this so that my joy may be in you and that your joy may be complete. My command is this: love each other as I have loved you. Greater love has no one than this: to lay down one's life for one's friends. You are my friends if you do what I command. I no longer call you servants, because a servant does not know his master's business. Instead, I have called you friends, for everything that I learned from my Father I have made known to you. You did not choose me, but I chose you and appointed you so that you might go and bear fruit – fruit that will last – and so that whatever you ask in my name the Father will give you. This is my command: Love each other.
>
> (John 15:7-17)

Mark's Gospel: the story of discipleship – the challenge of being a follower of Jesus

There are many ways of reading Mark's Gospel, and a host of themes and ideas that are particularly important to the author in his account of the life, ministry and death of Jesus. Nevertheless, it is recognised among scholars that Mark wrote it as a challenge for true discipleship. Mark was writing in the early second half of the first century when Christians were enduring intense persecution. So, following Jesus was not a fashionable choice, or a culturally inherited default position. Following Jesus as a disciple meant an intentional heart, a life of sacrifice and a deep grasp of the justice, peace and joy of the kingdom of God.

Mark's Gospel presents Jesus introducing a message of a radically new kind of kingdom of which he is King. It is a kingdom that is a reverse of typical empires. It is one where the poorest and the least are lifted up, where those in bondage are set free, and where mercy and forgiveness are more important that obtaining what you think you deserve. At the heart of this kingdom is suffering and humility rather than power and status. The Messiah is a servant, a Son of Man, and a beloved child, instead of a celebrity with letters after his name and an award-winning podcast. (Although, let's face it, his teaching is way better, more popular and more profound than any podcast). Finally, the Servant-King will be tried, tortured and killed rather than succeeding to the throne through an exciting revolutionary military coup. He is the sacrificial Lamb whose body is broken and blood is shed so that his people may escape bondage and go free.[4]

Throughout Mark's account the people around Jesus are challenged to decide what they think about him and his message. He is so contrary and mysterious, his words and actions so bewildering, that being a disciple takes a great deal of soul-searching, talking, attempting, working and a rethinking of just about everything. Discipleship of Jesus in this Gospel is not simply a moral lifestyle option. It is about teaching and learning and being formed from the inside out; a process of personal transformation and societal transformation – made all the more complex as it straddles politics, family,

4. For a good overview of the gospel see https://bibleproject.com/guides/book-of-mark/ (accessed 30.10.25).

work and religion as well as massive spiritual powers and realities too!

Mark manages to crank up the pressure and dynamism of all this by writing his account as if it's rushing by at an incredible pace. Not only are we taken from one surprise to another, from an exorcism to a parable to a death threat to a crowded sitting room, but it all happens 'suddenly' and 'straight away' with no chance to draw breath.

Mark doesn't duck the fact that Jesus lived life fully – and everything in life, the whole 360 degrees of it, is infused with his love and passion. Which is why, when he is asked what the greatest commandment is, he quotes Deuteronomy 6, followed by Leviticus 19:

> 'The most important one,' answered Jesus, 'is this: "Hear, O Israel: the Lord our God, the Lord is one. Love the Lord your God with all your heart and with all your soul and with all your mind and with all your strength." The second is this: "Love your neighbour as yourself." There is no commandment greater than these.'
>
> (Mark 12:29-31)

Jesus shows here that wholehearted sacrificial love is the essence of being a disciple. Love for God, love for yourself – or those you are already in family with – and love for your neighbour; that's anyone else, regardless of whether or not they are like you, for you, or with you. It is how he lived – up the mountain in prayer, in the house with his disciples and his new family, and out in the villages, towns and cities among both the poor and the powerful.

Discipleship is wholehearted: everything, everywhere, all the time.

Deuteronomy: Moses' call to everyday discipleship, a covenant of faithful, God-soaked love, that requires a brand-new heart

In the first part of Deuteronomy, Deuteronomy 1 – 11, Moses tells the story of the Exodus – the rescue and journeying of Israel. And on hearing this recounted, the listeners' question might be 'Why us?' It is because God has a loving ambition for this often grumbling, messy, recalcitrant rabble. He wants them to be a holy nation, an example of the good life, what it means to be at one with God, each other and the rest of creation. In Exodus 19:6, God says that he would like Israel to be 'a kingdom of priests and a holy nation'. This desire is then repeated all through Deuteronomy;[5] God is looking for a family who will be characterised by love, right living and the presence of God. This will then be noticed by everyone else in the world, and they too will want to join in and experience the same blessing.[6] This is the outward dimension of being a witness and serving the world around them. In this way, the people of Israel are called to be disciples just like Jesus' twelve were, and for the same reason. To receive, experience and then give away the love of God.

The way that Israel can become a 'holy nation', a 'treasured possession' (Exodus 19:5), with fame and honour and praise, is to love God with all their heart, soul and strength. Moses preaches his heart out about obeying the commandments, how much God loves Israel, what happened when they ignored God before and how much he wants to give them an amazing life in the promised land. All this is summed up in Deuteronomy 6:4-6, the theme of this book:

---

5. See Deuteronomy 4:37; 7:6; 26:19; 28:9; 29:13; 33:3.
6. Deuteronomy 4:6-8.

> Hear, O Israel: the LORD our God, the LORD is one. Love the LORD your God with all your heart and with all your soul and with all your strength. These commandments that I give you today are to be on your hearts.

Moses' teaching is nothing if not wordy. It must have taken him ages to write this huge farewell speech of Deuteronomy. But these words, these laws, commandments and statues, have no power unless they live in the heart. This is the essence of Moses' teaching. Following God is all about character and love – and obedience will be the natural outcome of such a heart. Therefore, for Moses, it is love for God that comes first for a disciple:

> The LORD your God will circumcise your hearts and the hearts of your descendants, so that you may love him with all your heart and with all your soul, and live.
>
> (Deuteronomy 30:6)

The middle section of the book is all about how to live well together, Deuteronomy 12 – 26. This is the 'love one another' aspect of discipleship. It covers matters of worship, integrity, leadership, responsibility. There are ways of living that respect the land, animals, family and neighbours. It addresses matters of justice and criminality, war, domestic relations, immigration, poverty. In fact, there is a broad sweep of ways of living that will shape a stable society, economy and spiritual identity. Not only, then, is this about one another, the family of believers, it also shows how we must love our neighbour as ourselves. Our witness is not simply gospel sharing in terms of words and a call to spiritual rebirth. It is how we go about looking after those we know and those we do not know. The outward mission that Moses describes is rather like Jesus' outward mission that he modelled for his disciples. It is about physical, mental, social and spiritual health. It is about economic and societal injustice being addressed.

The final section of Deuteronomy is back to the heart, Deuteronomy 27 – 34. After all the teaching and commandments that will help Israel be good disciples and followers of God, Moses re-emphasises that the true test of discipleship is whether we will follow with heartfelt trust and obedience. Will Israel choose life or death, blessings or curses?[7] Therefore the laws he has just spent so long defining are not going to make Israel holy. They will simply help Israel from straying into destructive patterns and will strengthen the cohesion of the people. Instead, he defines the nature of Israel's relationship with God as a covenant – which is a two-way commitment of love and trust.

For Moses, being a follower, a disciple, a true Israelite, is being one who has a pure and loving heart.[8]

One who is wholehearted.

You can find all the resources, links and information about the contributors mentioned throughout the book at www.springharvest.org/resources/no-greater-life/

7. Deuteronomy 30:19-20.
8. Deuteronomy 30:1-2,6,10,14,17,46.

Artist: Helen Yousef

PART ONE

Wholehearted

No Greater Life than following the Greatest Commandment – how to live life to the full in God's world, God's way

> 'Hear, O Israel: the Lord our God, the Lord is one. Love the Lord your God with all your heart and with all your soul and with all your mind and with all your strength.' The second is this: 'Love your neighbour as yourself.' There is no commandment greater than these.
>
> (Mark 12:29-31)

The great commandment leads to a great life. It is all about having a heart that loves to the full – God, one another, and everyone else, too! The love that Jesus describes is passionate, real and fully engaged. It is also a love that is not confined to religion or self-focused improvement. Loving God wholeheartedly means in prayer, family, friends, work and service. It is in our sitting, walking, lying down and rising up. To be a follower is to passionately love God and to love like God. It is a love that comes from and encompasses every part of who we are – heart, soul, mind and strength.

This first section of our exploration of the Great Commandment looks at its breadth and energy – 3D, 360 degree, 365 days – there's no greater life than following Jesus like this.

Classroom

Love God – Jesus quotes from Deuteronomy 6

In Mark 12, Jesus is quoting first of all from Deuteronomy 6:4-6:

> Hear, O Israel: the LORD our God, the LORD is one. Love the LORD your God with all your heart and with all your soul and with all your strength. These commandments that I give you today are to be on your hearts.

'Hear, O Israel' is important and we will examine that phrase later on in this section. The first thing we 'hear', though, is 'The Lord our God, the Lord is One.' There are a variety of emphases that scholars have given to this. Rather than this being about the philosophical essence of who God is, the *New International Commentary* and the Bible Project both lean towards the emphasis being that God is the only God for us to worship.[9] He is unique and omnipotent and this call is to follow him by devoting ourselves wholeheartedly to him, rather than to any of the other 'gods' that offer false hope, or to our own egocentric ways, or even to people we love or fear.

> Being a disciple is to wake up each day and choose again to follow Jesus – surrendering to the power and presence of the Holy Spirit as we seek to know Him, become like Him, and join in with what He is doing in the world.
>
> (Matt and Amy Summerfield, Zeo Church Hitchin, Reboot Your Leadership, Kyria, Skylark International)

9. Peter C. Craigie, *The Book of Deuteronomy*, NICOT (Grand Rapids, MI: William B. Eerdmans, 1995), pp. 168-169, https://bibleproject.com/articles/what-is-the-shema/ (accessed 30.10.25).

We are then called to love fully. We often separate our heart as where our feelings are, from our mind which is where our thoughts are, our soul which might be the spiritual bit of us, and then our body which we drag around to hold in all this metaphysical sense of being. Hebrew thought is that as human beings, we are more unified than this. The 'heart' (*lev*) is the centre of who we are, the place of intent, will, thinking and purpose. The 'soul' (*nephesh*) is who we are as a human: our body, our personhood, our vitality. The 'might' (*meod*) is our strength – but not just physical strength, it is our exertion and commitment; we might say our 'muchness' or our 'everythingness'. In fact, these three definitions in Deuteronomy 6 are actually different perspectives on who we are as one person, and each builds on the other. (One commentator says they are 'semantically concentric'.[10] Which sounds great – if you have a dictionary to hand!) Heart, soul and strength means who we are, in our entirety, as a living, breathing, decision-making, feeling, thinking person.

It is noticeable that Jesus' version of this passage in Mark's Gospel – which is written in Greek with dialogue first spoken in Aramaic – has another word added: 'mind'. This is complicated further by the fact that the scribe who responds to Jesus in agreement misses out the word 'soul'. Matthew's version of what Jesus says misses out 'strength'. Luke's version, which is a lawyer speaking but agreed with by Jesus, has the same words as Mark but in a different order. And the Septuagint, the Greek version of the Hebrew Bible that Mark and Jesus would have known, is a bit more fluid across versions but has the word 'power' not 'strength'. That is all quite complicated!

10. R. Laid Harris, *Theological Wordbook of the Old Testament* (Chicago, IL: Moody Press, 1999, c. 1980), p. 487.

Greek thinking separates the human person into different parts. The mind, the body, the heart, the soul: these would have been seen in Greek culture as connected but very different. The mind and thinking being elevated and the body being devalued, for instance. As noted above, Hebrew thought is more unified. We are 'living beings' (Genesis 2:7). Our hearts are where we think. Psalm 139:23 famously says: 'Search me, God, and know my heart; test me and know my anxious thoughts.' Solomon is told to 'serve [God] with wholehearted devotion and with a willing mind [*Nephesh*], for the Lord searches every heart and understands every desire and every thought' (1 Chronicles 28:9).

Mark, the Gospel writer, therefore is making it quite clear to both a Greek-thinking audience and a Jewish one, that Jesus is emphasising the full meaning of the Deuteronomy command. The mind is absolutely included in our wholehearted devotion to God, as much as what we now might think of as our feelings

> That verse just hits different when you let it sink in. Jesus isn't messing about – He's telling us what life's really all about. Loving Jesus with everything you've got, and loving people like they matter. That's it. That's the call. That's the life. There's no greater one. To me, loving Jesus with all your heart, it's not just something you say – it's something you live. It's about relationship, not religion. And the more I've walked with Him, the more I see that it's about going on believing, going on following, going on loving. Eternal life isn't just something you wait for when you die – nah, it's something you step into now, by the power of the Holy Spirit. It's a whole new way of living.
>
> (Gram Seed, Sowing Seeds Ministries)

or our spirituality. And Mark and Luke both emphasise how strength and mind go together. We might describe this as determination, since our mind can prevent us from doing what we could or should do. In light of this, perhaps we can begin to reorientate our own understanding of our hearts, so that we also see how our hearts are where our deep thinking and purpose reside, and our mind and strength is where the focus and determination is directed. In fact, having all these different Gospel writers have a stab at explaining this massively important command from God, and coming at it from slightly different angles, just goes to show how wide, broad, deep, and high is not only the love of God for us[11] but also our love for him.

It is also worth reading this slowly and carefully so that we see that Jesus repeats 'all your . . .' each time.

All of your heart
All of your soul
All of your mind
All of your strength

> For me, spiritual formation is the intentional investment of time, discipline, and energy into deepening my relationship with Jesus. Spiritual formation, in many ways, is about cultivating a heightened awareness of God's presence throughout my day. God is always present, but often, I am not present to Him. By pausing, quieting my mind, slowing my breathing, and redirecting my thoughts to Him, I create the space to truly be with God.
>
> (Brian Heasley, 24-7 Prayer)

11. See Ephesians 3:18.

Love God with everything you are and have and hope for, all the time, everywhere.

Love your neighbour as yourself – Jesus quotes from Leviticus 19

The second part of this great commitment is where Jesus is quoting from Leviticus 19:18:

> Do not seek revenge or bear a grudge against anyone among your people, but love your neighbour as yourself. I am the LORD.

This comes in the middle of a list of commands that are all about acting justly and kindly to those around you. It has also been noted by scholars that in Hebrew it literally says love 'to' the neighbour rather than a more benign having love 'for' the neighbour. This shows that love here is not a feeling but an action. It is then repeated towards the end of the chapter, but this time specifically about foreigners: Verses 33 and 34:

> When a foreigner resides among you in your land, do not ill-treat them. The foreigner residing among you must be treated as your native-born. *Love them as yourself*, for you were foreigners in Egypt. I am the LORD your God.
>
> (my emphasis)

This shows that 'as yourself' does not mean people like you, but means that the way we love others should be the way we love ourselves.[12]

12. For a helpful essay on the Golden Rule in the Bible, by Old Testament Professor John Collins see www.thetorah.com/article/love-your-neighbor-how-it-became-the-golden-rule (accessed 30.10.25).

Here in Leviticus the people might be excused for just loving one another; then loving a foreigner who has now settled and is living as one of them. When Jesus is asked about this in Luke 10, he tells the story of the Good Samaritan. This character would be someone who is a regional neighbour to be avoided, and a person who has not settled and adopted the same thinking and ways as Jesus' hearers. Jesus agrees with the questioning lawyer that the one who shows love (mercy) – even to a person so different from themselves – is the true neighbour. Showing mercy is what a Son of David does.[13] It is the ultimate act of royal kindness and the epitome of humanity acting at its most glorious. Jesus even goes so far as to say love your enemies, do good to them, pray for them – see Matthew 5:43-44 and Luke 6:27,35!

In Romans 5:8-10 Paul says twice that fulfilling this one command in Leviticus means you are fulfilling the whole law. He then repeats this assertion in Galatians 5:13-16. James calls this a fulfilment of the 'royal law' in James 2:8. This law is generally now known as the 'Golden Rule' and is found in

> Being a disciple means saying yes to Jesus and being willing to be obedient in following him. Of course, following Jesus will stretch our faith, challenge our mindsets, and recalibrate our priorities, but it is also the path of living abundantly! Discipleship means intentionally developing rhythms and practices where we allow the Word of God to shape us, we experience the Spirit's guidance and encounter his presence as we follow his truth daily.
>
> (Cathy Madavan, Speaker and Author)

13. 1 Samuel 24; 26; 2 Samuel 9; Psalm 51:1; Mark 10:47-48.

many religions and philosophies. Many of these are described negatively: do not do to others what you would not like them to do to you. But Jesus' version is unequivocally positive and intentional. His law is the law of practical, demonstrative love, that comes from devotion to God.

The Greatest Commandment is about our wholehearted, fully comprehensive love for God and also love for the people who are like us, as well as love for those who are different, far away, in need, and even against us.

No Greater Life is 3-Dimensional: Up, in and out

As we see Jesus put these two commands together, we notice that the love which is commanded is three-way. It is for God, for one another, and for the rest of the world.

> Jesus went up on a mountainside and called to him those he wanted, and they came to him. He appointed twelve that they might be with him and that he might send them out to preach and to have authority to drive out demons. These are the twelve he appointed: Simon (to whom he gave the name Peter); James son of Zebedee and his brother John (to them he gave the name Boanerges, which means 'sons of thunder'), Andrew, Philip, Bartholomew, Matthew, Thomas, James son of Alphaeus, Thaddaeus, Simon the Zealot and Judas Iscariot, who betrayed him.
>
> (Mark 3:13-19)

Jesus' 360-degree God-focused life was rooted in his everyday, and the stuff of earth as well as somehow connecting to heaven and the supernatural. And it was all done in relationship with his heavenly Father, with the people around him, and with those he had come to serve and save. Relationships are at the heart of this 360-degree life and it has been pointed out by many writers and Christian leaders that these relationships are so comprehensive because they are three-dimensional.

These three dimensions can be described as Upward, Inward and Outward.

Jesus went up the mountain in Mark 3 (described by Luke in his Gospel, 6:12, in order to pray the whole night alone). For Mark, places are significant – mountain, seaside, sea, synagogue, temple etc. The mountain is the place to meet with God, and Mark's readers would have immediately made this connection. In fact, this phrase 'went up [the mountain]' is mentioned countless times in Exodus to Deuteronomy, mainly about Moses when he meets with God. (And this exact Greek phrase of Mark's, occurs eighteen times in the Greek Hebrew Bible). So, for Mark, this story is about Jesus, the Son of Man,

> For me, key discipleship practices are: Active and tangible love: Living out faith by actively showing love in practical ways rather than just understanding it. Family-centered faith: Engaging in family prayer, devotions, and discussing faith together. Life-on-life discipleship: Engaging in deep, intentional discipleship within small groups. Empowering others: Consistently empowering others and giving away the best ideas, roles, and influence, training others, and encouraging succession. Servant-hearted partnering: Focusing on serving others and growing God's Kingdom rather than building one's own organization. Mentoring: Fostering a culture of mentoring and walking 'alongside' leaders.
>
> (Alan Charter, Children Everywhere Walking With Jesus)

demonstrating the need and desire for the *upward dimension* of worship, prayer and intimacy with God. Mark then writes that Jesus calls those whom he wanted 'and they came to him' (v. 13). Not only is Jesus a true disciple of the Father but he shows that he, too, is divine and the disciples come up to him in the same way that he comes up to the Father. The mountain is the place of prayer, worship and encounter with our glorious God. We are formed as disciples as we engage with God in these ways and practices; the Holy Spirit sanctifies us. Upward encounters of worship, prayer, revelation and amazement continue as a theme in Mark, often on a mountain.[14]

Mark then writes that he appointed the twelve to 'be with him' (v. 14). In between coming up the mountain to encounter God and then going out to preach God's message with power, Jesus emphasises the call to be with him and one another. This is the *inward dimension* of friendship, learning together, and sharing responsibility, resources and authority. Moses was given the law when he was up the mountain so that the people of Israel would be formed into a holy community, preparing them to be a witness and example to all the nations

> Being a disciple in everyday life, involves seeking to actively living out your faith and obeying God's commandments. It is lived out best in the context of family and community. Jesus gave a picture of family being those who obey His commandments. Being a disciple is not merely about understanding but actively shaping who we are and those around us through our faith.
>
> (Alan Charter, Children Everywhere Walking With Jesus)

14. Mark 4:39; 5:15,37; 6:46; 8:29; 9:2; 13:3; 14:32.

around. The most well-known word in the New Testament for this is *koinonia* – meaning mutually sharing community, having all things 'in common' (Acts 2:44). We typically call this 'fellowship', 'membership', or 'partnership'. It is as we live, love, and learn together that we become more like Jesus. In relationship with one another we are tested and refined, challenged and provoked. Our faith is then proved and improved by community. This kind of togetherness around Jesus is highlighted many times by Mark as the disciples often withdraw with Jesus to learn, process and share together. This, too, is formational.[15]

After Jesus calls the disciples (literally now 'named apostles', or sent ones) to be with him, Mark records the disciples' calling as being sent out to preach and cast out demons. To be sent is definitely an *outward dimension*! The idea is not that they stay physically up the mountain, or even physically together as twelve disciples, but that the experience of their upward call and inward call remains with them even as they are sent out. They carry that same spirit, holiness, instruction and relationship, so that others will know it too, by hearing and experiencing it. The preaching is the message they have received, and the casting out of evil is the power they have been given. To preach is to be a herald, to 'proclaim' with authority something that has already been done. So they don't

> Being a disciple is to extend compassion and support to those whom he loves – including the marginalized, the incarcerated, and the homeless – and to grow personally through the process of serving others.
>
> (John O'Connor, Junction 42)

15. Mark 1:29; 2:14,15; 3:13; 4:10,34; 6:30-32.

have to be clever speakers, simply witnesses who say what they've seen and heard. Jesus described this outward sending of himself from God by quoting Isaiah 61:1-2, recorded in Luke 4:14-21. Jesus was anointed to 'proclaim' the favourable year of the Lord – with good news, freedom, sight and release. This also is formational for us. As we do what Jesus did – both in relationship with God but also with the wider world – we become channels of his grace and power. Inevitably, this flow of life within and through us shapes and defines us. Our inner and outer behaviours imitate Christ and make us more like him. The outward dimension is spiritual, physical, social and psychological: the good news of Jesus covers all of human experience and is seen many times in Mark's Gospel.[16]

Formed by Jesus for what?

The disciples are being encouraged to pattern their lives on Jesus. But this forming is not simply so that they are good disciples who can follow a way given by their Master. It is because Jesus lives the greatest life ever. He is the perfect human and his example of love and service, where he is secure, satisfied and knows his significance in God the Father's eyes, is what he wants for all of us. We are learning as disciples so that we, too, can live like this. Following Jesus in these three dimensions is not just a daily regime. It actually changes us. The habits of discipleship change us '. . . to be conformed to the image of his Son' (Romans 8:29). We become like Christ, who lived the greatest life, and so there's no greater life to be lived than the one that Jesus offers.

> His divine power has given us everything we need for a godly life through our knowledge of him who called us by his own glory and goodness. Through these he has given

16. See Mark 1:32-34.

> us his very great and precious promises, so that through them you may *participate in the divine nature*, having escaped the corruption in the world caused by evil desires.
>
> (2 Peter 1:3-4, my emphasis)

Jesus is the Son of Man, the shape of living, the one-of-us. His call is to rule and reign with him – not domineering but looking after one another and the whole of creation. 'You have made them to be a kingdom and priests to serve our God, and they will reign on the earth' (Revelation 5:10). This is the goal of our discipleship – to be like Jesus and to join him in his eternal living.

Wholehearted: Following the Great Commandment

The kind of inward, upward, and outward discipleship that Jesus demonstrates for us is way more practice than theory. This is the nature of the Greatest Commandment, and this

> To be a disciple in everyday life means following the example of Jesus. He lived the human experience as our living Torah, the tangible expression of what it means to be fully human before God. In him, we see the Word in action embodied in compassion, obedience, and love. Discipleship, then, is about embodying that example in our own lives. It is asking each day: How do I love the Lord my God? How do I love my neighbour? To be a disciple is to live out those questions faithfully, drawing from the life of Jesus as our guide.
>
> (Sammy Jabangwe Hanton, The Message Trust)

relational emphasis of being face to face, living in the everyday, and embracing real life, is seen in the words of Moses in Deuteronomy, and the words of Mark in his Gospel.

> 'Not all of us can do great things. But we all can do small things with great love.' – Mother Teresa of Calcutta.[17] Like most people, my everyday life isn't lived in the highlights, it is made up of the hidden, the repetitive, and the mundane. The things I do every day aren't big in the eyes of the world: I look after my children and our home, I do life with my family. I do not get paid for this, so in the eyes of the world, I do not even 'work' . . . and yet, I'm hardly idle. Many small things my husband and I do add up to a home where the children feel safe and loved, and have their first taste of what God is like as we try to model grace, mercy and justice all at the same time (and I'm definitely in need of God's wisdom to know which of these to model when!) St Josemaria Escriva said, 'Holiness does not consist in doing more difficult things every day, but in doing them every day with greater love.'[18] It is not that difficult to do what I do. And at the same time, on my own, I can't do it! I need to keep close to God for wisdom and strength, and to infuse the things I do with Kingdom love. Why? Because the stakes are so high: two precious, immortal souls entrusted to us, to form them towards a love of God and to pray them into his kingdom (and that's a big responsibility we as parents carry and must not neglect), and besides all that, we need to teach them how to adult.
>
> (Susanne Willdig, Open Ears: Speech to Text)

17. www.goodreads.com/quotes/6946-not-all-of-us-can-do-great-things-but-we (accessed 6.11.25).
18. https://opusdei.org/en-uk/article/working-conscientiously/ (accessed 6.11.25).

Following the Great Commandment in Deuteronomy (Deuteronomy 5:1-6; 5:29-6:9)

The first part of the Great Commandment that Jesus is quoting is from Deuteronomy 6:5. This is part of the big speech Moses starts in chapter 5 where he gathers the people of Israel and shares with them the Law of God, including the ten commandments, in order that they can live well in the promised land. Therefore, it is worthwhile looking at the way Moses introduces the Greatest Commandment, and the kind of language, ideas, stories and laws he highlights on the way. This will give a good idea of what it meant for Moses to be a wholehearted disciple of God.

> Moses summoned all Israel and said:
>
> *Hear, Israel,* the decrees and laws I declare in your hearing today. Learn them and be sure to follow them. The LORD our God made a covenant with us at Horeb. It was not with our ancestors that the LORD made this covenant, but with us, with all of us who are alive here today.
>
> (Deuteronomy 5:1-3, my emphasis)

> To me, discipleship is about living a life that ultimately centers around Jesus Christ. Even in the everyday rhythms of family life or work that falls outside of a church setting, the pursuit of Jesus as King remains the underlying goal and prayer. It's easy to get distracted by the 'noise' of life – don't get me wrong. But when it comes to the big decisions and the long-term direction, the guiding question is always: How can we best serve God and become more like Jesus?
>
> (Philippa Hanna, Singer Songwriter)

'Hear' means not just to listen but to truly hear, understand and put into practice. It is the words *shema* and *shama* in Hebrew, and it is also the word that is used for 'obey' (e.g. 'To obey is better than sacrifice', 1 Samuel 15:22). There is a twice daily prayer in Jewish tradition called 'The Shema'. This includes these verses as well as similar ones in Deuteronomy 11:13-21 and Numbers 15:37-41. The Shema is prayed because it is about a covenanted and repeated desire to be wholehearted in devotion to God and for this wholeheartedness to be about every aspect of daily life, will, desire and behaviour. It is not just about religious belief or even other-worldly spirituality: it's a hearing that leads to doing; Bible verses of instruction and teaching that are actually put into practice all the time. That is discipleship! I was told of one rabbi who used the rhyming phrase Shama is a Hammer. It forms and shapes, it re-forms and trans-forms. It beats smooth and knocks off the rough edges. This is a how a silversmith takes some rough silver and fashions it patiently and lovingly into a beautiful item. A number of times, the Bible uses images of silver being tested and refined to describe the forming that God does with his people to make them pure.

> The Lord spoke to you *face to face* out of the fire on the mountain . . . And he said: 'I am the Lord your God, who brought you out of Egypt, out of the land of slavery.
>
> (Deuteronomy 5:4-6, my emphasis)

Face to face is up close and personal. These instructions in Deuteronomy are not a dusty manual, or even like remote controlled CCTV for the smooth running of a motorway or a town. This kind of learning and living is about a relationship with God, hearing God's words, and experiencing the passionately reasoned 'why' that sits behind his teaching. This is the 'why': God is the personal rescuer – he saved Israel from slavery because he loved them.

Face to face is how a parent and baby make their loving and trusting connection. We see the 'apple' of the eye – literally in Hebrew this is 'the little man' or 'daughter' of the eye – probably because we see a tiny reflection of ourselves in the child's pupil (Psalm 17:8). This is intimate, and it is how God sees us. 'I will be a Father to you, and you will be my sons and daughters, says the Lord Almighty' (2 Corinthians 6:18).

Face to face is also how lovers see one another, gazing into each other's eyes. This is highlighted in Song of Songs as a description of human love but also a glimpse of the love that God expects to have with us: 'You have stolen my heart, my sister, my bride; you have stolen my heart with one glance of your eyes' (Song of Songs 4:9). Hagar, in Genesis 16:13, is the first person to give God a name, and it is because she experiences his loving gaze upon her: 'She gave this name to the LORD who spoke to her: "You are the God who sees me," for she said, "I have now seen the One who sees me."'

> One of the most helpful and also challenging practices I have found on this journey of formation is *stillness*. As Thomas Merton once said, 'In order to spiritualize our lives and make them pleasing to God, we must become quiet.'[19] Learning to pause, even briefly, throughout the day has been a difficult but crucial discipline for me. I have to work hard at this practice. This means that sometimes, I hold a small object like a cross or a stone to help me focus, or I quietly repeat a Bible verse in my mind. Other times, I find stillness by gazing at a piece of art or simply observing the world around me. I've even experienced moments of stillness in the chaos of a crowded train station during rush hour – just by sitting down, getting myself in the right headspace and asking Jesus to reveal himself to me.
>
> (Brian Heasley, 24-7 Prayer)

19. https://embodygrace.org/2010/04/26/thomas-merton-on-asceticism-and-sacrifice-part-2/ (accessed 6.11.25).

Face to face is how friends are with one another – not a master and their slave, or a divine being and their creature: 'The Lord would speak to Moses face to face, as one speaks to a friend' (Exodus 33:11).

> Oh, that their *hearts* would be inclined to fear me and keep all my commands always, so that it might *go well with them* and their children for ever!
>
> (Deuteronomy 5:29, my emphasis)

Moses then recounts the giving of the Ten Commandments, the foundation of the teaching of God for his people, Israel. And then we come to the heart of how God sees his children and followers of his ways. Which of course is all about our hearts. When our hearts are aligned with God's heart, with the way that Jesus lived and talked, then we are blessed – we experience wellbeing, the good life, contentment – the

> If I'm honest, the noise and demands of life often disturb this stillness, agitating me and threatening to steal it away. When this happens, I try to name those distractions and frustrations, bringing them into the light. In doing this I surrender them to Jesus, acknowledging my flawed humanity with its competing desires and appetites, and allowing his grace to quietly flow into me. In doing this, stillness helps to recentre my scattered senses, refocus my desires, and restore the balance I so deeply need as a disciple of Jesus.
>
> Stillness is often the fertile ground in which spiritual formation begins to take root. It is there that I rediscover the truth: in Jesus, I have enough.
>
> (Brian Heasely, 24-7 Prayer)

promises of the Beatitudes in Matthew 5. This is where circumstances may be hard, and worldly expectations unfulfilled, but there is the promise of heaven's richness, mercy and grace – 'theirs is the kingdom of heaven' (Matthew 5:3). This is what it means for it to go well with us and our children.

> But you stay here with me so that I may give you all the commands, decrees and laws you are to *teach them to follow* in the land I am giving them to possess.
>
> (Deuteronomy 5:31, my emphasis)

'Teach' and 'Follow' literally means to 'learn' and 'do'. It is what an apprentice does, a student, a disciple. It implies watching closely and copying the teacher. Moses is being asked by God to make disciples.

> So be careful to do what the LORD your God has commanded you; do not turn aside to the right or to the left. *Walk in obedience* to all that *the LORD* your God has commanded you, so that you may live and prosper and prolong your days in the land that you will possess.
>
> (Deuteronomy 5:32-33, my emphasis)

My 'Making Disciples' definition of discipleship is this: Discipleship is loving and obeying Jesus with your head, heart and hands. Discipleship has to be thought about as apprenticeship to the way of the kingdom of God. Jesus apprenticed his followers in the craft of the kingdom and not as a teacher of sound theology. So rather than discipleship being something we learn in a classroom, Jesus operated as a master craftsman who apprenticed his followers to imitate him in this supernatural work.

(Cris Rogers, Spring Harvest, All Hallows Church Bow, Making Disciples)

'Walk in obedience' – this literally means to 'walk in the way/road'. The way of Yahweh (the LORD) is introduced in Genesis 18:19 where God speaks about Abram (who, like Moses in Exodus 33:11, is described in James 2:23 as 'God's friend'):

> For I have chosen him, so that he will direct his children and his household after him to *keep the way of the LORD* by doing what is right and just, so that the LORD will bring about for Abraham what he has promised him.
>
> (my emphasis)

This is pretty much the same as being said by Moses here in Deuteronomy. And then it is seen in the opening of Mark's Gospel, 'Prepare *the way* for the Lord' (Mark 1:3, my emphasis) and modelled by Jesus who walked on the road in obedience and called people to follow him on 'the road' (Mark 10:52); who was himself '*the way* and the truth and the life' (John 14:6, my emphasis). Discipleship can be described, therefore, as a Way: a pathway, a way of life, a set of habits. In fact the first disciples in Acts were called followers of 'the Way' (Acts 9:2). For Moses, the Way described the whole forty years journey of the Israelites in the desert. Not only was it a physical journey with challenges, miracles, drama and battles, but it was the journey that took a group of Hebrew slaves and formed them into a people who were God's holy nation. Spiritual formation is not a single decision or an event, but it is a Way made up of habits, rituals, obstacles and breakthroughs, and how our heart, soul and strength deal with that.

> These are the commands, decrees and laws the LORD your God directed me to teach you to observe in the land that you are crossing the Jordan to possess, so that you, your children and their children after them may fear the LORD

> your God as long as you live by keeping all his decrees and commands that I give you, and so that you may enjoy long life. Hear, Israel, and be careful to obey so that it may go well with you and that you may increase greatly in a land flowing with milk and honey, just as the LORD, the God of your ancestors, promised you.
>
> (Deuteronomy 6:1-3)

We have seen how the way of Yahweh for Moses and the people of Israel was a literal journey in the wilderness as well as a journey of cultural formation as God's people followed closely the cloud, fire and voice wherever it went. Likewise, Mark's Gospel is the story of Jesus' missional journeys and his way of life. Mark shows Jesus' call to people to come close and follow him in their way of life, and in so doing, to become like him.

Following the Great Commandment in the Gospel of Mark

Mark's stories are of people who worship, follow, struggle and rebel – so similar to the Moses narrative. This time, it is disciples he calls, individuals he encounters; vicious opponents and demanding family. From a rich young ruler to a poor widow; from Bartimaeus who jumped up and followed, to 'everyone deserted him and fled' (Mark 14:50). Following Jesus

> As much as possible I try to be attentive, obedient, and consistent. A prayer that I often pray is, 'Keep me far from compromise and lead me towards compassion and bring me into closer communion with you, Lord Jesus.'
>
> (Robin Vincent, Care for the Family)

is a theme of Mark's and this is defined as hearing, loving and obeying the promise of God for us to become like Jesus. Mark shows this happening as people spend time with him, learn from him as a group of disciples, and then practise, declare and demonstrate his kingdom.

The beginning of discipleship happens when people come close to Jesus or Jesus calls them to himself, as we see in Mark 1:40 and 10:42. The emphasis in Mark is on making room for people to get close rather than preventing them and keeping them at lecture-style distance. Those who come to touch Jesus – children, a bleeding woman, a Gentile woman, a blind man, the woman at Bethany, and of course 5,000 people on a hillside – are often rebuked or hindered. But Jesus welcomes and enables this. He likes to be face to face, however awkward this may be at times. We may look at him and turn away with our faces sad, like the rich young ruler in chapter 10, because we do not feel we can truly follow Jesus. Or we may look with pride and scorn and spit on him like the teachers of the law in chapter 14. His invitation is to join him, whoever we are and whatever our faith or lack of faith looks like. 'And we all, who with unveiled faces contemplate the Lord's glory, are being transformed into his image with ever-increasing glory, which comes from the Lord, who is the Spirit' (2 Corinthians 3:18).

As part of my DMin I realised that the structure of Mark's gospel is that of an apprenticeship model. Right from the first call we see the structure from 'I do, you watch, we talk', to 'you do, I help, we talk', to 'you do, I watch, we talk', and then to 'you do, someone else watches'.

(Cris Rogers, Spring Harvest, All Hallows Church Bow, Making Disciples)

Both Mark's Gospel and Deuteronomy are showing how true discipleship is about being wholehearted, up close and personal, and following Jesus and Yahweh on the Way. They each define what a Great Life looks like by demonstrating that the commandment to love is for God, for their own people and for the world they are called to be witnesses among.

Living Room

There is no greater life than an ordinary life filled with the extraordinary Holy Spirit

When we were looking at the immediate context of the great commandment in Deuteronomy 6, we didn't quite get to the end of the section. But what comes straight after the commandments fits very well in Living Room, because it is all about applying these commands to everyday life.

> Impress them on your children. Talk about them when you sit at home and when you walk along the road, when you lie down and when you get up. Tie them as symbols on your hands and bind them on your foreheads. Write them on the door-frames of your houses and on your gates.
>
> (Deuteronomy 6:7-9)

This is firstly about talking. Sharing our faith and belief, being open with the way we understand the Bible, prayer and our relationship with God. The best experiences of church are generally where we find a group of people we can do this with. It is always good to worship together and to engage in missional activities and projects, especially to serve others. But the depth of church life comes from having a few people who will gather round Jesus, read the Bible, pray and look after one another spiritually as well as socially and practically. Even a good small group or life group in church can become a calendar item, an event to attend, an activity that goes alongside Sunday worship, regular giving, and being on a rota. Look at what Moses says about how these commands should be embedded in our lives . . .

Sit in your house, walk by the way, lying down and rising up

'Sitting in our house' is us when we are at our most unguarded – where we can be ourselves and not have to put on an act for anyone. This is where we can talk about Jesus, love him and feel his presence. You may have been into certain homes that feel very peaceful, or friendly, or godly. That is because faith is expressed and lived out there as much as at church. It doesn't remain in the privacy of someone's head but is chatted, normalised and so becomes part of the atmosphere.

'Walking by the way' is a great phrase that sums up our daily activity – going to work, or shopping, to the cinema, or out with the dog. The rhythm of walking is like the rhythm of prayer. It is constant, steady, purposeful and becomes unconsciously part of who we are. Jesus-centred spirituality that is as present when we go about our daily lives as it is in a prayer meeting or worship time is seamless. There really should be no difference in our passion and awareness of God when we are in the supermarket as there is when we are pouring out our hearts in sung worship. And likewise, our worship life should be as accessible and authentic to others as any other activity we do.

> I'd say being a disciple in the everyday is about living from a posture of surrender – choosing Jesus in our thinking, our reacting, our speaking, and our serving. It means walking closely with Him when no one is watching, and allowing that relationship to shape how we show up in every sphere of our life.
>
> (Arianna Walker, Mercy Ministries)

'Lying down and rising up' emphasises time and routine. It includes the most restful aspects of our lives and the most purposeful. Everything about our lives is inspired by the word of God. In Deuteronomy 8:3 Moses says that the whole point of the forty-year journey in the wilderness was 'to teach you that man does not live on bread alone but on every word that comes from the mouth of the Lord'. Jesus quotes this when he resists temptation to avoid including God in negotiating the needs and opportunities of life, in Matthew 4:4. It is clear from his life that Jesus' own rising up and lying down was enjoyably and seriously soaked in the Word of God, even when the rising up was to face his captors in Gethsemane and the lying down was in the middle of a life-threatening storm on Galilee.

Hand, head, doorposts and gates

How do we fill our hearts with love for God and his word? Moses here has a tangible suggestion – to bring God's Word into our everyday lives so that it is close as possible to where we are and how we live. There are Jews who take these commands very seriously indeed and their response is literal. They have God's words stored in little boxes (phylacteries) that they attach to in their heads and arms. They store God's Word in a small cylinder attached to their doorposts and gateways.

We may also take this literally and have posters on the walls, sticky notes on fridge doors, notifications each morning on our phones and tattoos on our wrists. Being reminded of God's Word is so helpful, which is why we may do reading plans, listen to Lectio 365,[20] and have a liturgy that takes us through the day with Scripture and prayer.

Most probably these words are hyperbole – they are telling us how important it is to have God's Word close in every sphere of our lives – hands, heads, homes and communities.

20. https://lectio365.com/ (accessed 31.10.25).

Our hands are how we do things – menial, sacred, professional, recreational, and caring activities. We lift up our hands in worship and reverence for his word, whatever we are doing.

> Let us examine our ways and test them, and let us return to the LORD. Let us lift up our hearts and our hands to God in heaven . . .
>
> (Lamentations 3:40-41)

Our forehead is where our brains sits – our thoughts and reactions to all that is going on around us should be filtered through our love for God. It is also the bit between our eyes – everything we see we can look through the lens of God's Word as we lift our eyes upward to him.

> I lift up my eyes to you, to you who sit enthroned in heaven . . . so our eyes look to the LORD our God, till he shows us his mercy.
>
> (Psalm 123:1-2)

Our doorposts represent our homes, where we are with family and friends. Every time we welcome someone into our house, we can share our love for God with them. They are also the place of security. We have alarms, CCTV and ringdoorbells today. God, however, encourages us to be protected by his word.

> Being a disciple, for me and for those I support, is about inviting the kingdom of heaven into every part of our lives: body, spirit, and soul. That includes how we care for ourselves. It's about aligning every area with God's truth and allowing Him to shape our thoughts, actions, and choices daily.
>
> (Gaynor van der Burton, FitFish)

As for God, his way is perfect:
The LORD's word is flawless;
he shields all who take refuge in him.

(Psalm 18:30)

Our gates are where we connect with the wider world. In the Bible, gates were where city decisions were made. Trade happens in gateways. Therefore, the way we relate in business, politics, recreational and community life should be defined and shaped by the Word of God.

Blessed are those who listen to me,
watching daily at my doors,
waiting at my doorway.
For those who find me find life
and receive favour from the LORD.

(Proverbs 8:34-35)

For the purposes of our theme:

Hand and Heart may well represent our **upward devotion** to God.

Our Doorposts, our **inward devotion** to one another.

Our Gates, our **outward devotion** to our neighbourhood, town, country and world.

> I love how Romans puts it: take your everyday ordinary life & place it before God, I love the supernatural God weaves into our everyday ordinary to make it supernaturally ordinary every day!
>
> (Dan Hargreaves, Alive Church Lincoln)

Up, in and out

This is quite easy to remember. Three very short words, describing three relationships. Love God, Love One Another, Love the World

Some people use a triangle to describe it.

See this helpful video from 3DM: 'How to teach the 3dm triangle in a huddle'.[21]

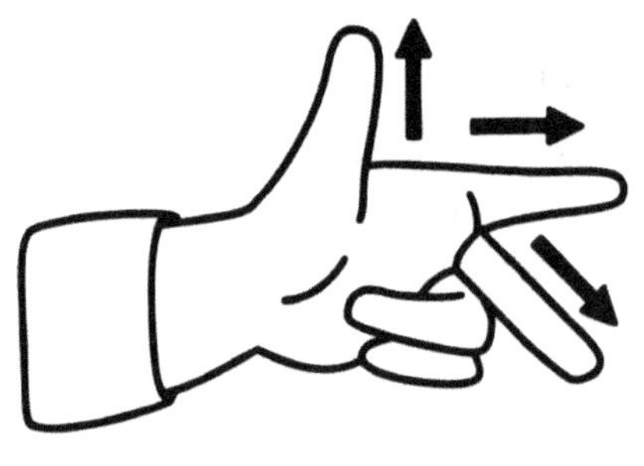

You can use your hand, too. The thumb sticking up represents the upward dimension. The middle finger, pointing to the left or right, is the inward dimension, the second finger points away, as the outward dimension. (The physicists among us will get distracted by Motion, Field and Current at this point; the rest of us won't have a clue about that.)

Another image might be a wine-skin, or barrel, or even bottle.

Jesus talks in Mark 2:22 about a new wineskin for the new wine of his gospel. It needs to be filled with new wine, needs to hold and mature the new wine, and needs to pour out the new wine.

21. www.youtube.com/watch?v=Y6W5KUFogmE (accessed 30.10.25).

The upward dimension is the need to be filled – to *embrace and be embraced* by the love of God. When we worship and when we pray; when we deliberately lift our eyes up to God to love, serve and honour him; then we can be filled with his Holy Spirit. This happened dramatically to the first apostles as they prayed in Acts 2:4 and 4:31.

> Living for Jesus isn't just something we do on Sundays – it's our way of life. As directors of The BIG Sing choir, we see every rehearsal, performance, and conversation as an opportunity to live out our faith in practical ways. In our work with The BIG Sing, we believe God has given us a platform to reach hearts through music. Many people walk into our choir rehearsals or concerts not expecting a spiritual encounter – but we know God meets them there. We've seen people in tears during a gospel song, sharing afterwards that they felt something shift inside. That's the Holy Spirit at work. We may not always preach from a stage, but every lyric, every note, and every smile is a seed being sown. In the wider community, we've made it our mission to bring hope where there's been isolation, unity where there's been division, and joy where there's been despair. Whether we're singing in schools, care homes, prisons, or public spaces, we carry Jesus with us. Ultimately, living for Jesus means being available – saying 'yes' when he calls, showing up with love, and letting Him use our lives as a bridge between the Church and the community. And through the choir, we've seen countless moments where God does just that.
>
> (Howard and Gemma Francis, The Big Sing)

The inward dimension is where the new wine and the wineskin or barrel mix with one another over time. The wine takes on flavours and matures, and even improves. The new wine of the kingdom is about God's Spirit mixing with the spirits of people, men and women, seen most beautifully of course in Jesus, the Son of Man, and the result is the most perfect taste of heaven and earth. This is where we are *encouraged* and *equipped*.

The outward dimension is when the wine is poured out. It is no good just sitting there, only ever improving with age or becoming more expensive. Prophetic wine connoisseurs in the Bible have advice on this: drinking aged wine is recommended by Isaiah (25:6) and not doing anything with it is condemned by Jeremiah (48:11). The Spirit of God was poured out on all humanity in Acts 2, and it looked like the disciples, who were not as posh or refined as Isaiah and Jeremiah, were drunk on it! They *extended* out the love of God to all those around them – even to 'the ends of the earth' (Acts 1:8).

A wineskin needs to be able to receive, hold and pour the new wine. In the same, we embrace with love, encourage and equip with love, and extend with love. We need to be filled, be sanctified and be sent out as anointed ambassadors, sommeliers, wine tasters, baristas – those who invite others to the feast and carry the aroma of that feast wherever we go.

> My artistic practices are woven into my faith practices. Most mornings, I wake early, make tea, and go to a space I've made beautiful – a candle, a comfy chair. I stream-write my morning pages, read scripture, and pray. It's quiet, grounding, and sets the tone for my day, whether I'm heading to the studio or leading an adult art workshop. There are no rules – if I miss a morning, I don't feel guilty. It's not a duty, it's a joy. A habit.
>
> (Debs Last, Artist)

Practising the Way

In his excellent book on discipleship, *Practicing the Way*,[22] John Mark Comer sums up being a disciple as this: 'Be with Jesus, Become like [Jesus] and Do as he did'.

This is such a simple and helpful way of expressing what it means to be a Christ follower. As we think of a three-dimensional life, one that is upward, inward and outward, then it is easy to see how John Mark Comer's observations work in practice.

The best way to *be with Jesus* is in our worship, prayer and reading of the Bible; our conscious walk with him. This is the upward dimension and it will be both a solitary and corporate experience. And as we do this, we are not only with Jesus but we become like him. There are ways and habits that help us to be with Jesus. When we are with him, we are filled with his Spirit.

Becoming like Jesus is possible! But it means being with him, showing love to others, and also continued practice. We can train our minds, bodies and hearts to allow the Holy Spirit to mould and shape us so that we become more like Jesus. Being with Jesus, and then deliberately becoming like him – on our own and also with others – changes our character and affects our behaviour. Together, we naturally demonstrate love, oneness and what good family can look like, which is the inward dimension.

Being with Jesus and becoming like him inevitably means that we also intentionally put love into action for the sake of others – near and far – especially those who have been mistreated, excluded, or broken by their own or others' behaviour. When we *do as Jesus did*, we can create a wonderful community of kindness. This is inevitably seen and experienced by those who don't yet

22. Colorado Springs, CO: WaterBrook Press, 2024.

know Jesus. They are impacted by our transformed character and Christlike behaviour. The welcome, words, works and wonders of Jesus are what we do as the outward dimension of our *faith*.

Wholehearted: A story

I remember as a student going away with other Christians for a weekend. It was stimulating, faith-filled and a tantalising taste of the living power and excitement of God's Word and Spirit. There was also something dodgy with the mushroom soup. I came back on a coach with that furred-up tongue you get when your stomach is upset, and a whole load of cigarette smoke blowing around to add to the feelings of ash in the mouth. (How I miss those days of smokey clothes and confined spaces . . .) I got back home feeling really queasy and sat in a chair sipping hot water – as my mum had always told me to do when I was a child and felt sick. I put on some worship music – maybe like a charm to ward off the nausea. Eventually, however, I got up, rushed to the toilet and wretched over the bowl; that out-of-control, body-contorted seizure, with mouth open rictus wide and nothing really coming out, apart from a long dribble of bile.

> Being a disciple in our everyday life is to repeatedly, and actively, choose to take a step away from the distractions of life and to step toward Jesus. It's to follow and to learn; to fall and get up again; to constantly shift our priorities to ensure he is at the top. It's realising, as we take those crucial steps to follow in Jesus' blueprint for life, that He doesn't walk ahead with us trailing behind . . . but that he instead walks alongside us.
>
> (Bethan Newman, Youth for Christ)

I was hot, clammy and feeling absolutely awful. But then I experienced what felt like a shower of love from God – all through my body and mind. It was as if he were saying to me, 'I love you, Martin.' And at that moment, half bent over, clutching the cistern lid, I said out loud, 'And I really love you, Jesus!' The feeling of being loved and saying to God how much I loved him, soon replaced that sweaty wretchedness. I went and sat back down, slowly and gingerly, but I actually felt so very good.

This is what it is to be loved by God – to know body, soul, mind and strength that you are loved. And to be able to cry out in return – with that same body, soul, mind and strength – 'I love you, God!' Being filled with the Holy Spirit is not always experienced in a physical or even emotional way, but because of the way we are 'wonderfully made' (Psalm 139:14), quite often our response to the love of God involves the whole of who we are. The grace of Jesus ignites in us the desire and ability to begin to live out the Greatest Commandment; and in doing so, to inherit a truly great life.

What is your story of experiencing the love of God, or what would you like it to be?

Artist: Ruth Hearson

Playground

For all the resources, links and information about the contributors mentioned, scan the code to visit:

www.springharvest.org/resources/no-greater-life/

Practices

Throughout each Playground section of this book there will be a prayerful Bible reading example from Lectio 365, which is a prayer app from 24-7 Prayer. Download for free to pray the Bible morning, noon and night. You can also follow their free online course that teaches how to pray the Bible in ancient and new ways at: The Lectio Course, www.24-7prayer.com/resource/lectio-course/

Resources

An excellent guide to the Bible, in a way which opens up its patterns, themes and teachings is The Infographic Bible by Karen Sawrey. For those who enjoy processing in a non-neuro-typical way, Karen's approach is full of images, statistics, illustrations and charts. This makes sense of worship in the Hebrew Bible, for instance, or the emphasis given by each gospel writer to various teaching themes of Jesus. Even the feel of the paper and the colours used reflect the Bible's intricate glory. It is a fascinating and incredibly worshipful and mindful tool for the disciple of Jesus. See www.theinfographicbible.com

Praying Scripture

Can you memorise Jesus' commandment in Mark 12?

> 'The most important one,' answered Jesus, 'is this: "Hear, O Israel: the Lord our God, the Lord is one. Love the Lord your God with all your heart and with all your soul and

with all your mind and with all your strength." The second is this: "Love your neighbour as yourself." There is no commandment greater than these.'

(Mark 12:29-31)

Lectio Divina 1

The Way of Love
Mark 12:28-34

Let's pause and pray with a Lectio 365 Morning Prayer, meditating on the moment when Jesus showed us the most important thing we can do as Christians.

Together we will pray (P.R.A.Y.): P – pausing to be still, R – rejoicing with a psalm and reflecting on Scripture, A – asking God to help us and others and Y – yielding to his will in our lives.

Pause

As I enter prayer now, I pause to be still; to breathe slowly, to re-centre my scattered senses upon the presence of God.

Pause and pray

Prayer of Approach

As I become aware of your presence in this place and time,
Open my eyes to perceive you,
Realign my mind to believe you,
And reawaken my heart to receive you,
Now and throughout the day to come.

Rejoice and reflect

I choose to rejoice in God's love today, joining with the ancient praise of all God's people in the words of Psalm 5:

> But let all who take refuge in you rejoice;
> let them sing joyful praises forever.
> Spread your protection over them,
> that all who love your name may be filled with joy.
> For you bless the godly, O LORD;
> you surround them with your shield of love.
>
> (Psalm 5:11-12, NLT)

Pause and pray

Jesus is in the temple debating with the religious leaders and experts. In this passage I reflect on his response to a particularly challenging question . . .

> One of the teachers of the law came and heard them debating. Noticing that Jesus had given them a good answer, he asked him, 'Of all the commandments, which is the most important?'
>
> 'The most important one,' answered Jesus, 'is this: "Hear, O Israel: the Lord our God, the Lord is one. Love the Lord your God with all your heart and with all your soul and with all your mind and with all your strength." The second is this: "Love your neighbour as yourself." There is no commandment greater than these.'
>
> 'Well said, teacher,' the man replied. 'You are right in saying that God is one and there is no other but him. To love him with all your heart, with all your understanding and with all your strength, and to love your neighbour as yourself is more important than all burnt offerings and sacrifices.'

> When Jesus saw that he had answered wisely, he said to him, 'You are not far from the kingdom of God.' And from then on no one dared ask him any more questions.
>
> (Mark 12:28-34)

In the temple, the very place where sacrifices were offered, Jesus explains that his way – his kingdom – is about much more than attaining personal holiness. Out of the 613 laws captured in the Old Testament, Jesus makes his priorities clear. The commands to love God and to love my neighbour may be found in different parts of the Torah, but by elevating them above all others, Jesus declares that love comes first.

Ask

Am I fully focused on loving God with all my heart, all my soul and all my strength?

Lord, I want to fall deeper in love with you. Is there something other than you that I am devoted to? Something that is unhelpfully capturing my heart, distracting my soul and directing my strength?

Pause and pray

Who is the neighbour I am particularly called to love today? I invite the Holy Spirit to bring to mind someone I can share God's love with practically and personally.

Pause and pray

Yield

As I return to the passage I look out for a particular word or phrase that the Holy Spirit seems to be highlighting to me today.

> One of the teachers of the law came and heard them debating. Noticing that Jesus had given them a good answer, he asked him, 'Of all the commandments, which is the most important?'
>
> 'The most important one,' answered Jesus, 'is this: "Hear, O Israel: the Lord our God, the Lord is one. Love the Lord your God with all your heart and with all your soul and with all your mind and with all your strength." The second is this: "Love your neighbour as yourself." There is no commandment greater than these.'
>
> 'Well said, teacher,' the man replied. 'You are right in saying that God is one and there is no other but him. To love him with all your heart, with all your understanding and with all your strength, and to love your neighbour as yourself is more important than all burnt offerings and sacrifices.'
>
> When Jesus saw that he had answered wisely, he said to him, 'You are not far from the kingdom of God.' And from then on no one dared ask him any more questions.
>
> (Mark 12:28-34)

I take a moment to reflect on any word or phrase that the Holy Spirit is highlighting for me.

Pause

I'm struck by the phrase, 'no one dared ask him any more questions.' Jesus' response silenced those who had been testing him.[23] Their questions had been complex and detailed, but Jesus made it clear: knowledge alone isn't the way to enter the kingdom of God. How can I better engage my heart in my pursuit of God today?

Pause and pray

23. Mark 12:13.

Yielding Prayer

Holy Spirit, would you lead me into the greater depths of love for you? 'Create in me a pure heart . . . and renew a steadfast spirit within me' (Psalm 51:10).

Yielding Promise

And now, as I prepare to take this time of prayer into the coming day, the Lord who loves me says in 1 Corinthians:

> Go after a life of love as if your life depended on it – because it does.
>
> (1 Corinthians 14:1, *The Message*)

Closing prayer

Father, help me to live this day to the full,
being true to you, in every way.
Jesus, help me to give myself away to others,
being kind to everyone I meet.
Spirit, help me to love the lost,
proclaiming Christ in all I do and say.
Amen.

Lectio 365 is a prayer app from 24-7 Prayer. Download for free to pray the Bible morning, noon and night.

Further Bible verses to read and reflect on

1 John 2:4-6; 1 Chronicles 28:9-10; Genesis 26:3-5

Journal – pray, reflect, write

Be with Jesus. Become like Jesus. Do what Jesus did.

How do I spend time with Jesus, and what do I need to do to give more of my time to be with him? Are there some practices or habits that will help me to do this in my busy life?

....

....

....

Am I becoming like Jesus? When I look back over the last six weeks of my life, have I changed? Has the word of God altered and shaped me at all? What is my testimony – my recent story of Jesus at work in me?

....

....

....

What things am I doing that Jesus did (apart from raising the dead and casting out thousands of demons)? Am I teaching others about the love of God? Am I allowing myself to be interrupted so I can serve a need? Am I withdrawing when necessary but also deliberately engaging? Am I being with my friends, worshipping with others, praying on my own?

....

....

....

 Reflective prayer

Read the hymn words 'Take my life and let it be' – read and read again as a prayer: www.hymnal.net/en/hymn/h/445

 Action

Design a life of wholehearted love.

What can you do to build in wholehearted devotion for God into your life and context?

For example:

- House dêcor, clothes, food;
- Planned conversations and rituals as family and friends;
- Serving the needs of the poor or cultivating and tidying the environment in your community as an act of love for God.

 Group Bible study

Each Bible study will contain two contrasting stories of discipleship. These stories will demonstrate how the call to discipleship demands passion, commitment and faith. There will be an example that Mark gives us of wholehearted discipleship (often from people who are not even officially called disciples (typically women, outsiders and ill people), and a contrasting example of discipleship that ends up missing the point or even opposing Jesus.

A tale of two wholehearted encounters

Read Mark 5:21-43:

- Who are the 'disciples' we are meant to notice and imitate in this story?
- What does the attitude and behaviour of both Jairus and the woman tell us about their hearts?
- How and why does Mark highlight the physicality of feet, hands, touch and pressing in?
- Talk about the attitude of the disciples and Jairus' people in verses 31,35,38,40. When and why do we also respond like this?
- What do we learn from Jesus' response in verses 32,36,39-40?
- Share together about the times you have pleaded earnestly, been vulnerable, heard about Jesus and acted on it, been in fear and trembling about your actions.
- Share together about the times you have laughed, been cynical, derided, mocked, and so have stopped believing.
- Talk about any resolutions you may make in the light of these two deliberately intertwining stories.
- This is a story of gained opportunities and potentially missed opportunities. Pray together about hearts that pursue and receive Jesus.

Wholehearted – a series of studies about the heart #1

This book is all about the heart – the heart of a disciple of Jesus.

There is so much in the Bible about our hearts.

What we are like on the inside.

How holy we are, or empty, or mean, or compassionate, or broken, or devoted, or divided, or pure.

The Bible says that sin and death have hardened our hearts; they have become like stone.[24] That means they are so dense that nothing of God's words and ways can properly soak into them. Of course, as humans, we can still feel – both love and hate – but essentially our hearts are spiritually dead and on life-support while we live on the earth. God's salvation plan is to give each of us a heart transplant so that we can apply our passion to the goodness, truth and beauty modelled for us by Jesus Christ, and continue this, increasingly, forever.

---

24. Ezekiel 11:19; 36:26.

> I will give them an undivided heart and put a new spirit in them; I will remove from them their heart of stone and give them a heart of flesh. Then they will follow my decrees and be careful to keep my laws. They will be my people, and I will be their God.
>
> (Ezekiel 11:19-20)

The Hebrew word for heart is *leb*. It is made up of two letters, *lamed* and *bet*, בֵּל.

Lamed looks like a shepherd's crook or cattle goad. (Hebrew reads from right to left.) So it represents the idea of a goad or a prick to ensure that we follow instruction and go in the right direction. It is a picture of learning, and the word *Lamed* comes from a root word meaning teaching and learning. It is also the tallest of the Hebrew letters and is the middle of the alphabet so it is the 'heart' of the Hebrew alphabet and points upwards the way to God.

Bet is the second letter of the word *leb*. You can see that this looks a bit like a house or tent with a side opening; a picture of earthly dwelling. It represents what is inside.

Put these two letters together and we can see that the heart is where our learning and instruction from God lives within us. The heart is where we have true wisdom – deep knowledge of who God is, filling us up on the inside, abiding in us, and so, very naturally, directing our steps, choices, responses and intentions. Our heart is a home for God's understanding; a temple for him to rule from.

Dr Julie McKinley who leads the work of Bible Society in Ireland comments specifically for this section of our book:

> There are a lot of mystical thoughts around *leb* – in the ancient world it wasn't as much the seat of our emotions, that was more the kidneys, but more our mind and thoughts/intellect – there doesn't seem to be the separation in Hebrew between our mind and heart that we experience in the Western world. There is a beautiful connection with the letter *lamed*, which itself means teaching (*talmid* is one who learns/students or a disciple, and the Talmud is just 'learning'), where the rabbis understand the letter itself as an acronym, Lev Mveen Daat (L M D as Hebrew is a consonantal language), which means 'a heart that understands wisdom/knowing'. The idea behind this is that the goal of Torah learning is to absorb its teaching's deep into one's heart, like Deuteronomy 6, 'these words shall be upon your heart . . .', as they are upon it they begin to seep in, like rain upon the soil.

Being a disciple, then, is being a learner – one whose inner house is receptive and open to the teaching and purpose of God. The book of Deuteronomy is all about teaching and learning. Its title literally means second or repeated teaching. It is all the experience that Moses had gained, crafted and designed into something like the Alpha course, that he could teach the people of Israel – and all who followed after them.

It is not surprising, then, that the word heart crops up many times throughout this teaching – because that's where Moses is hoping that all his instruction, given by God, will find its home.[25] And in a hope-filled prophetic way, the word for heart – that is used throughout the book as the place to receive and live out God's teaching – is extended slightly. It is *lebab*. It has the letter *lamed* – teaching, and the letter *bet* – tent, and then an additional letter *Bet* added at the end. Scholars tend to agree that both words, *leb* and *lebab*, are used relatively synonymously for the idea of heart. The first can also emphasise the physical organ whereas the second seems to concentrate on the feelings, intentions, thoughts and will that settle there. Perhaps, though, that repeated letter *Bet* emphasises that the heart really is a home. Or that a Spirit-softened, Spirit-filled heart is both a home for us and a home for God.

Mark's Gospel, too, is all about the heart. Usually Jesus is observing – as we saw in those verses from Ezekiel earlier – that people's hearts are often hardened.[26] They are closed to the transformative power of Jesus' words and actions. His mission in Mark's Gospel is to live a life of a full and softened heart and see how this attracts or repels people. The chosen disciples are often the ones with hardened hearts, and they lack understanding. But those who come to Jesus in humility, sorrow and desperate hope are the ones who Jesus says have faith. They are the ones who follow and obey his wise instruction instinctively and joyfully.

---

25. Deuteronomy 4:9,29,39; 5:29; 6:5 etc. – more than forty times!
26. Mark 3:5, 6:52, 8:17, 10:5.

Discipleship, then – following both Moses and Jesus – is all about the heart.

Not just feelings, although they certainly play their part – but the word of Christ dwelling richly in us, the peace of Christ ruling our hearts.[27]

Our hearts are the place of thought, deed, passion and purpose.

Our home and God's home.

> For this reason I kneel before the Father, from whom every family in heaven and on earth derives its name. I pray that out of his glorious riches he may strengthen you with power through his Spirit in your inner being, so that Christ may dwell in your hearts through faith. And I pray that you, being rooted and established in love, may have power, together with all the Lord's holy people, to grasp how wide and long and high and deep is the love of Christ, and to know this love that surpasses knowledge – that you may be filled to the measure of all the fullness of God.
>
> (Ephesians 3:14-19)

Questions

Can you describe to one another how you first came to 'know' Jesus? What took place in your head and heart at that time – whether it was an event or a process? How are you convinced about who Jesus is in your life?

---

27. Colossians 3:16.

We often say that we 'open our hearts' to Jesus – either in this first instance of conversion or the journey of trust, or in specific moments of prayer and worship and contemplation. Think through, or if you are in a group, talk together about what that looks like in your life – how do you 'open your heart'?

When you read or listen to the Bible, or hear someone speaking about the Bible, have you ever had the experience where you would say that God is speaking to you? Is there a difference between that and simply thinking about something? If you are with others, share times when you have felt this happen to you.

What are the Bible verses that you know deeply? The ones that you not only can recite, but they have meaning for you? Share these important meanings with one another if you are studying this as a group.

Pray (for each other) to be alert to hear the voice of God through Scripture.

Artist:
Scott Moles

By the blood and sacrifice Jesus made for us all, I often can't believe this was done for me, Me being made anew, healed, purified and forgiven brings me to my knees in thankfulness. Romans 12:2 about being transformed and a renewing of the mind. Identifies to me I can change and be renewed daily.

The picture I designed is all about this, and the journey I went on. The words on the back are part of this. The love Jesus must have for me is undeniable. And I'm so very thankful for.

(Scott Moles)

PART TWO

Up The Mountain

Looking up:
to love Jesus in our worship

Classroom

The first dimension of wholehearted discipleship is Up. This is our worship to God. It is interesting that Jesus says the Greatest Commandment is to love God, from Deuteronomy 6:5. Earlier in his ministry Jesus has rebuked the devil by quoting from a few verses later in Deuteronomy 6:13, where Moses says, 'Fear [or revere] God, [and] serve him only' (Matthew 4:10).

Therefore, love, reverence and service are all linked together.

So, what is worship and why do we worship?

Instinctively we tend to worship what is excellent. Admiration and respect for sports and entertainment stars, as well as cultural leaders, easily grows into adulation and sacrificial honouring. We also bow the knee to what we think has power to help or hinder us. Throughout history, people have worshipped gods of various sorts, and religion has been one way of working out why things go right or wrong in life, and how we might try to influence that.

As a Christian, however, I want to worship God because he is God and I am not. God is excellent in every way. God made the universe. God does all things well. God holds everything

> We encounter the presence of God through both attentive and disruptive practices. In attentive practices, we experience 'God in the slow' – soaking in spiritual habits like Scripture, prayer, fasting, worship, and stillness. In disruptive practices, we meet 'God on the go' – posturing our hearts to be ready for the everyday interruptions where we notice what God is doing and join in.
>
> (Matt and Amy Summerfield, Zeo Church Hitchin, Reboot Your Leadership, Kyria, Skylark International)

in his hands. God's character and capability are so good and awesome that it is natural for us to praise him. I also want to worship God because Jesus has sacrificed his life in order to give me eternal life. This is worship of gratitude, deep dependence and thankfulness. There is no other power that can reach into death and redeem what has been lost, and so worship is the most natural and right response to such love.

There is also the upward movement of praise and worship that is inbuilt into creation. 'The heavens declare the glory of God' (Psalm 19:1). All the earth worships God, see Psalm 66:4; the earth, heavens, sea, fields and trees all rejoice, see Psalm 96:11-12), and the 'host' of heaven bow down (Nehemiah 9:6). This is because everything was made with, through and for Jesus. The whole of creation is the Father's gift to the Son. Everything points towards Jesus: the Alpha and Omega, 'author and perfecter' (Hebrews 12:2, NASB1995), Word of creation, redeemer and King.[28]

> He is the image of the invisible God, the firstborn of all creation. For by Him all things were created, both in the heavens and on earth, visible and invisible, whether thrones or dominions or rulers or authorities – all things have been created through Him and for Him. He is before all things, and in Him all things hold together. He is also head of the body, the church; and He is the beginning, the firstborn from the dead, so that He Himself will come to have first place in everything. For it was the Father's good pleasure for all the fullness to dwell in Him, and through Him to reconcile all things to Himself, having made peace through the blood of His cross; through Him, I say, whether things on earth or things in heaven.
>
> (Colossians 1:15-20, NASB1995)

28. Romans 11:36; 1 Corinthians 8:6; John 1:1-3; Hebrews 1:2.

We were made to worship Jesus, and one day, with all the heavens and the earth, we will join in the song: 'Worthy is the Lamb, who was slain, to receive power and wealth and wisdom and strength and honour and glory and praise!' (Revelation 5:12).

These are good reasons to worship: my recognition of greatness and excellence, my heartfelt gratitude and the innate calling to declare to Jesus blessing, honour, glory and dominion forever.

Worship is also a gift to us

Worship is not simply an activity that starts with us and ends up with God. Jesus' rebuke to Satan along with the many commands by Moses in Deuteronomy not to follow other gods[29] shows that worshipping God alone must also be a precious gift for us if it is so contested by Satan, our enemy. It is a wonderful mystery that could be missed entirely, or not fully grasped, even by a Christian.

We see in Jesus' teaching (especially in John's Gospel) about himself, the Father and the Holy Spirit, that God as holy and loving Trinity is the most wonderful experience. Jesus receives all his life, joy and purpose from this. God is not only the creator

> My recommended discipline is each day to put on 'Jesus-goggles', not 'beer-goggles' i.e. to seek to live with a Jesus-lens that filters everyone we see, everything we say, every action we take through the person of Jesus, who is perfect Love.
>
> (Simon Guillebaud, Speaker and Author, Great Lakes Outreach, Burundi)

29. Deuteronomy 4:19; 5:9; 8:19; 11:16; 13:2; 29:18; 30:17.

of the universe (which is pretty mighty!), but he is eternally in living relationships. He is love. And at the end of the day (certainly at the end of our days), it is love and relationship that matter more than anything in existence. Amazingly, the plan of God has always been that the people he made would get to experience this kind of trusting, perfect love, and enjoy all that God enjoys in himself: Father, Son and Holy Spirit.

James Torrance, in his book, *Worship, Communion and the Triune God of Grace* emphasises that the incarnation is a way of bringing us up into joining in with the life of God, the Trinity.[30] The first true act of worship was that of Jesus, offering himself fully to God in every way; trust, love, service and commitment from the perfect human being. In this he was honouring God as great, and thankful to God for his life. This was totally sacrificial, which shows us what's at the heart of worship. Jesus emptied himself on our behalf; took the sin and brokenness of the world, and was broken and became sin for us, triumphing over Satan in the surprising power of his pure humility. In worship we are emptied of false ego, but completed and perfected in Christ. We choose submission, and in doing so stand strong in the face of evil.

Jesus' worship was also that of the new Adam, a human who was totally involved in the loving relationships of God. Therefore, our worship is joining in with Jesus. Torrance says that worship is a gift of God so that through the Spirit we can join in the way that

> Discipleship is about demonstrating the love and teachings of Jesus through actions.
>
> (Rosie Giles, Spring Harvest)

30. James B. Torrance, *Worship, Community and the Triune God of Grace* (Menlo Park, CA: IVP, 1997), p. 32.

Jesus is in communion with his heavenly Father.[31] Worship is also a gift to us and not just our own response to God, obedient and right as that might be. That is why Jesus does not want it robbed by the devil, and why Moses keeps warning people not to worship other people, things or gods. Of course, this idolatry will pain God, but the pain is because he loves us so much and wants us to experience him, rather than be corrupted and destroyed by being formed by something less than God's good holiness. This is *agape* love – selfless and generous.

> Worship is an innate calling, an act of obedience, and a gift.
>
> Loving God is an innate calling, an act of obedience, and a gift.
>
> Serving God is an innate calling, an act of obedience, and a gift.

This gift elevates us from being creatures, slaves or even hired servants, to becoming friends. And the picture that is hinted at and then given finally in the Bible for this, in Revelation 19:7, is that of lovers who get married. Lovers are grateful for being chosen (like being picked for a school sports team) and are in awe of the person they are marrying (like getting an autograph from their idol) but the most special part of being married is loving and being loved.

The reason therefore for this commandment of Jesus is because it is right, and because its rightness is so good for us.

> Obedience is not a trial or a test to only be endured.
>
> Obedience is giving and receiving love.
>
> Obedience is worship and it is so good; it leads to a far greater life!

31. Torrance, *Worship, Community and the Triune God of Grace*, p. 20.

> The law of the Lord is perfect, refreshing the soul.
> The statutes of the Lord are trustworthy, making wise the simple.
> The precepts of the Lord are right, giving joy to the heart.
> The commands of the Lord are radiant, giving light to the eyes.
> The fear of the Lord is pure, enduring for ever.
> The decrees of the Lord are firm, and all of them are righteous.
> They are more precious than gold, than much pure gold; they are sweeter than honey, than honey from the honeycomb.
> By them your servant is warned; in keeping them there is great reward.
>
> (Psalm 19:7-11)

Looking up to God as Deuteronomy people

Most of the book of Deuteronomy (chapters 12 – 26) consists of rules and regulations for living life well. This huge sermon of Moses begins in chapter 12 with the where, why and how to worship God. Scholars observe that in Deuteronomy the most important way in which Israel should love the Lord their God is in their worship.[32] They are not to worship gods

> My habit is to study the scriptures each morning and to pray daily, so that I am continually transformed into His likeness and can reflect His glory to others.
>
> (John O'Connor, Junction 42)

32. For instance, Interpretation commentary series: Patrick D. Miller, *Deuteronomy* (Louisville, KY: Westminster John Knox Press, 1990), p. 129.

like the Canaanites did, doing whatever they think is right in their own eyes and only respecting the things they have made themselves. Instead, they will find the place where God chooses; they will be truly generous and sacrificial in their attitude; they will eat and rejoice, and invite God's presence into everything they put their hand to.

We will soon look at the helpful metaphor of mountains as a place where we can meet with God. In these instructions, however, it is not about the geographical *where* or the physical *how* humans think they should worship. Pagan worship of the time was about how the local peoples tried to reach God. But Yahweh, in Deuteronomy, takes the initiative, and in his eyes worship is determined by who he is and how he can reach people. Four times in chapter 12, God says it is all about the way 'he chooses' it should happen (seventeen times altogether in the whole book). This is not so much about a physical place – the sanctuary tabernacle was designed to be on the move, after all – but about creating space in personal and community life to meet with God, invite others in and experience his blessing. The most perfect example of a moving tabernacle where God lives is, of course, Jesus. John says Jesus 'made his dwelling among us' (John 1:14) which literally means he pitched his tent or tabernacled

> Sabbath rest has been an essential discipline to being emotionally and spiritually healthy. Taking time to breathe, rest and be with God. Alongside this, taking an extra day every now and again to go on a retreat. Either walking out in the country, or booking a room in a quiet space to sit and rest with Jesus.
>
> (Cris Rogers, Spring Harvest, All Hallows Church Bow, Making Disciples)

among us. Paul says Jesus was the 'spiritual rock' that followed the people of Israel (1 Corinthians 10:4). God wants to be among us, to be worshipped, for our sake more than his own sake.

In Deuteronomy, Mount Gerazim is the place from which blessings flow (Deuteronomy 11; 27), so when Jesus meets the woman at the well in John 4 she insists it is still this mountain that is the right place to worship rather than Jerusalem, which came late to the party. Jesus responds that worship is not defined by one special place – whether it's a mountain on which Moses worshipped, or a mountain on which King David worshipped. Instead, it is God who defines the what, where and how of worship because he intends it to centre round his Son, Jesus Christ, who will then pour out spiritual water from his innermost being to bless those around him. Morning or evening, Sunday or weekday, at home, at work, at church, in prison, in hospital, on holiday, at school, walking the dog – the God of Deuteronomy says: 'Let's enjoy each other here!'

Mountains and meetings

Throughout Scripture, mountains are often places where people meet with God. A mountain is where the earth touches heaven. Mountains inspire awe in us. The journey up is often hard but the reward is seeing afar and feeling somehow transcendent. It is not surprising, therefore, that in the Bible a mountain is where humanity and divinity meet. The most well-known event of the wilderness journey of the people of Israel is the giving of the Ten Commandments. Moses says: 'I went up on the mountain to receive the tablets of stone, the tablets of the covenant that the Lord had made with you' (Deuteronomy 9:9). This is Horeb, 'the mountain of God' (Exodus 3:1). This is a place of intense holiness, where God meets people – whether that is Moses at the burning bush or Israel receiving the Ten Commandments – and sets them on the journey of faith and discipleship. In an earlier story, it was on a different mountain, Mount Moriah, that Abraham met with God significantly when he showed he would even sacrifice his own son, Isaac.[33] This is the mountain that then becomes Zion, God's 'holy mountain' (Psalm 2:6), where God and his people meet and dwell together. One mountain brings destiny, calling and equipping. The other, fulfilment, living and being.

There are plenty of other mountain experiences with God where eyes are opened, faith is renewed and spiritual battles are won.[34] In Deuteronomy, mountains are also places where blessings and curses are known, written and proclaimed – where the promised land is surveyed and prayed over.

> For me, worship is the doorway. Singing – especially spontaneous worship seems to clear the fog. I'm lucky really because I regularly find myself in settings that demand that of me! And it forces me to immerse myself in the reassurance of God's Word. There's something about singing praise that aligns you with truth; the most powerful way to overcome lies. If you don't happen to be a worship leader, I highly recommend accepting those invitations to worship nights and events because they present such a valuable opportunity to be reminded of God's power and sovereignty. And don't forget, the car or living room can be great sanctuaries too.
>
> (Philippa Hanna, Singer Songwriter)

33. Genesis 22:2.
34. 2 Kings 6:17; 1 Kings 19:11; 1 Kings 18:20.

A mountain is a place of seeing and being seen. Seeing the presence of God, his word and will, the state of our own hearts, and the landscape that we are to conquer.

The most intense mountaintop encounter is when Moses meets God on Mount Horeb. This is recounted in Deuteronomy 10 but the detail of this in Exodus 34 is extraordinary. Moses meets with God who comes down in a cloud, causing Moses to bow and worship in Exodus 24:1-28. Moses then comes down the mountain and his face is so radiant because of meeting with God that the people are afraid![35] Similarly, the tabernacle is a place of encounter and face-to-face friendship where Moses pours out his heart to God, and God himself shares his own heart with Moses. Worship like this is where we experience the glory of God, we are drawn into a loving relationship with him, and we experience favour, grace, goodness, compassion, and rest.[36]

> To keep from getting bogged down in the daily practicalities, and to keep my eyes on doing the small things with great love, I keep a few practical stepping stones in my day.
>
> I have a watch that beeps every hour, on the hour. When I notice that beep, I take a breath and remember the Holy Spirit is right there with us, and that the purpose of it all is Jesus' love. I wear two rings on the 'wrong' hand: one for each child. They remind me to pray for them throughout my day. Whenever possible, I attend daily Mass – and I always offer up my children to Jesus on the altar. They are his first, and mine only for a time; and his heart is more committed to loving them than mine can ever be.
>
> (Suzanna Willdig, Open Ears: Speech to Text)

35. Exodus 34:29-35.
36. Exodus 33:1-33.

Meeting with God is totally transformational. God's holiness changes us. We see him face to face and hear his voice speaking to us. Everything in life is dull compared to this; black and white rather than technicolour. Yet in these kinds of encounters we are also invited to continue in our everyday lives with the expectation that God will be with us, that overcoming temptation and evil is possible, and that there is a life of fullness and satisfaction to be enjoyed.

> On this mountain the LORD Almighty will prepare
> a feast of rich food for all peoples,
> a banquet of aged wine –
> the best of meats and the finest of wines.
> On this mountain he will destroy
> the shroud that enfolds all peoples,
> the sheet that covers all nations;
> he will swallow up death for ever.
> The Sovereign LORD will wipe away the tears
> from all faces;
> he will remove his people's disgrace
> from all the earth.
>
> (Isaiah 25:6-8)

Looking up to Jesus in Mark's Gospel

Mark's Gospel has a number of mountain scenes and each of them shows Jesus looking upward in his relationship to the Father as well as people looking up to Jesus. Jesus also seeks wise life choices through seclusion and retreat. This reflects the journeying of the people of Israel in the wilderness as they either choose to love God and look up to him on that challenging journey, or look down and away to complaining and selfish decisions.

In fact, Mark's Gospel starts in the wilderness with the prophet John declaring that Jesus will baptise people in the Holy Spirit: the love of God 'poured out' within our hearts (Romans 5:5). Then Jesus retreats to the wilderness. Retreat is an important part of Jesus' rhythm in Mark's Gospel. He is seen quoting Deuteronomy when confronted with temptation. In Matthew's version of this episode, Jesus is taken to a high mountain to worship the devil but declares that 'Worship the Lord your God, and serve him only' (Matthew 4:10). In this private place, Jesus chooses to love God with all his heart. Similarly, he retreats to pray after a busy season caring for people and goes up the mountain to pray after feeding the 5,000.[37]

We have already noted that Jesus goes up the mountain (in Luke 12 to pray all night) to call his disciples to join him up there so he can from them into his community.[38] This is a story that is similar to Moses meeting God on the mountain and then teaching Israel the Ten Commandments. Another story that echoes this Sinai event is where Jesus 'led them up [Peter, James and John] a high mountain, where they were all alone' (Mark 9:2). He was transfigured before them, shining even more fully than Moses did, with Moses and Elijah there, too. And then a cloud and a voice (which are recorded with utter terror in Deuteronomy 4:33,36; 5:22-26) saying, 'This is my Son, whom I **love. Listen** to him!' (Mark 9:7, my emphasis)

> Listening to worship music really helps me to experience God's presence, and from there prayer flows out, and leads me to the scriptures where I experience even more.
>
> (Alexandra Huggins, Faith in Later Life)

37. Mark 1:45; 6:46.
38. Mark 3:13-19.

Listen and *Love*.

> *Hear*, O Israel: . . . *Love* the LORD your God . . .
>
> (Deuteronomy 6:4-5, my emphasis)

In a later section we will contrast this worship moment that is misunderstood by the three disciples, with another one in a house in Bethany in Mark 14. Bethany is not described as a mountain but it is a similar elevation to the Mount of Olives and Zion (you just have to go down and then up again to get to it!). The woman who breaks the alabaster jar and pours perfume over Jesus' head as an extravagant act of worship and devotion, while everyone else is harshly rebuking her, is commended by Jesus for her beautiful act. She somehow appreciates the sacrifice he is going to make on behalf of the world, and her response is to climb this mountain and break open her life in order to quietly, but bravely and generously, show her love for Jesus.

There are three more clear mountaintop experiences in Mark's Gospel. In Mark 13, Peter, James, John and Andrew are with Jesus on the Mount of Olives. They ask him about the future. His response is prophetic, not unlike the last chapters of Deuteronomy where Moses looks to the future where there will be challenge and uncertainty for the people of Israel. From this high vantage point, Jesus can see beyond his disciples' reality. When we worship and gaze at Jesus, we are also able to see and hear his words more clearly, about our lives now

> I love looking for opportunities in the everything . . . Each day asking God to reveal his plans, opportunities and then the courage to seize them.
>
> (Dan Hargreaves, Alive Church Lincoln)

and also where we are headed. Being up close and personal with Jesus in this way brings '[strength, encouragement] and comfort' (1 Corinthians 14:3). His 'words will never pass away' (Mark 13:31).

In Mark 14:32-42 Jesus is on the Mount of Olives in the Garden of Gethsemane. This mountain seems to be the place where he is most at home in the presence of God. He prays here, distressed and troubled. His soul, commanded in chapter 12 to love God, is 'overwhelmed with sorrow to the point of death' (v. 34). The upward dimension of Jesus' prayer, worship and love for God is real, honest and true. From this we learn that to love God is not always with feelings of happiness, or fun, or being carefree. Our love may be expressed in pain, doubt and vulnerability.

Finally, Jesus is crucified on Golgotha. This was a visible location shaped like a skull, probably elevated, outside of the mountain-rock city of Jerusalem. Jesus' supreme act of worship and obedient love for his heavenly Father was his sacrificial death. There is no greater love than to give your life for your friends, as we read in John 15:13, and therefore no greater life to be lived. It is on this isolated and despised mountain that we see how to love God with all our heart, soul, mind and strength.

Praise Him

What is praise? In their book *Praising and Knowing God*, David Ford and Daniel Hardy describe it as an 'ecology of blessing'.[39] God blesses his creation, honouring, respecting and delighting in it, which erupts in praise as it – sun, moon, stars, animals, plants, and humans – rejoices in being alive. This in turn opens

39. Daniel W. Hardy, David F. Ford, *Praising and Knowing God* (Louisville, KY: Westminster John Knox Press, 1985); David F. Ford, *Self and Salvation: Being Transformed* (Cambridge: Cambridge University Press, 1999), p. 156.

hearts to receive yet more blessing from the God who loves and is also loved in return. Blessing is overflow, more than enough, infectious and spirit-perpetuating. We can see this kind of praise in the worship life of Israel, and also in the way that Mark writes his Gospel about Jesus.

There is an order to the festivals and rituals that the Israelites are invited into. A year-round rhythm of thankfulness for Yahweh's personal love for them, a newly released and formed people: 'I am the Lord [Yahweh] your God, who brought you out of Egypt, out of the land of slavery' (Deuteronomy 5:6). Times are set in order to stop work and enjoy God, one another and life itself. And within this order, Ford and Hardy write that there is a 'non-order'. Laughter and energy, music and singing, feasting and dancing. Praise is like jazz. It has structure that is there to be played and experimented with, riffed on and explored. Making shelters out of branches every year would have been fun. Turning the work of farming into a community feast, animals, wheat, wine and oil, would have been chaotic, noisy and delicious. The smell of smokey (surely Southern-style) barbecue is mentioned forty times in the Bible as a 'pleasing aroma'[40] to the Lord – let alone to the people queuing up for their flatbread burgers, cooked by Aaron's gang of sous-chef priests.

> I recommend having priority to read the Bible and praying. Moving it from a discipline into a habit. But also – not just settling for just a morning and evening routine – trying to be immersed in the word and prayer as much as possible.
>
> (Nicky Wong, All Hallows Church, Bow)

40. Exodus 29:18,25,41.

> Celebrate the Festival of Tabernacles for seven days after you have gathered the produce of your threshing-floor and your winepress. *Be joyful* at your festival – you, your sons and daughters, your male and female servants, and the Levites, the foreigners, the fatherless and the widows who live in your towns. For seven days celebrate the festival to the LORD your God at the place the LORD will choose. For the LORD your God will bless you in all your harvest and in all the work of your hands, and *your joy will be complete.*
>
> (Deuteronomy 16:13-15, my emphasis)

> Come, let us *sing for joy* to the LORD;
> let us *shout aloud* to the Rock of our salvation.
> Let us come before him with thanksgiving
> and extol him with music and song.
> For the LORD is the great God, the great King above all gods.
>
> (Psalm 95:1-3, my emphasis)

> I delight greatly in the LORD;
> *my soul rejoices* in my God.
> For he has clothed me with garments of salvation
> and arrayed me in a robe of his righteousness,
> as a bridegroom adorns his head like a priest,
> and as a bride adorns herself with her jewels.
> For as the soil makes the sprout come up
> and a garden causes seeds to grow,
> so the Sovereign LORD will make righteousness
> and praise spring up before all nations.
>
> (Isaiah 61:10-11, my emphasis)

When God blessed the ark of the covenant while it rested at Obed Edom's farmyard, David experienced the overflow. He danced with all his might – fulfilling the great commandment

– not worrying what people thought of his self-abandonment (2 Samuel 6:16,22). And despite his wife's resentment towards his leaping, he threw in shouting, trumpets and sacrifices, and then spread out this praise widely by blessing all the people with what sounds like sticky toffee pudding and mince pies. Praise is loud, boisterous and delicious.

In Mark's Gospel there is no backstory of the birth of Jesus, as given in Matthew and Luke, nor a brilliantly dense theological and poetic sermon on who Jesus is, given in John's Gospel. Instead, Jesus explodes onto the scene. His introduction is that he is the Christ, the Son of God. He fulfils all Israel's history and he is the concentration of love and respect of God the Father and Spirit. The word 'immediately' is used eleven times in chapter 1 alone! People automatically leave everything and follow him (vv. 16-20). People are astonished and 'amazed' (Mark 1:22,27). Demons are crying out (vv. 23,26) and being cast out (vv. 26,34,39). The sick are healed (vv. 31,34,42). People are coming from everywhere and he is going everywhere (vv. 39,45). Chapter 2 and beyond carries on with more astonishment and people glorifying God.

My own discipleship journey has been helped by dedicating time to be alone with God; focusing on interacting with him through prayer, praise and scripture – being deliberate in inviting the Holy Spirit to guide me in those times. I also need a community of other disciples to support and encourage me, this includes my wider church family but also some closer individuals with whom I can have mutual accountability, reflection and growth (1 Thessalonians 5:11).

(Peter Wilson, Spring Harvest, Physiotherapist)

These are various translations and ways of interpreting reactions from the following two verses – Matthew 9:8; Mark 5:42: 'Filled with awe', 'glorified God', 'marvelled', 'astounded', 'astonished' . . .

Ford and Hardy highlight this explosion of praise and wonder, as well as the misunderstanding, opposition and bewilderment that whirls around the exorcisms, teaching and healings. Mark presents Jesus as one who demands a response – to be in awe and wonder and praise or to be angry and resentful at his brilliance and utter goodness. According to Mark, the authors say, Jesus' death is all about praise even in the face of suffering and death. And his resurrection – puzzlingly and sparingly told by Mark in the first few verses of chapter 16 – is the moment when awe and wonder, bursting through puzzlement and grief, will explode with such force that a few weeks later thousands of people will be filled with the Holy Spirit.

Praise is totally natural, full of energy, and connects us earthwards to creation and heavenwards to God. It looks backwards in thankfulness and appreciation but also looks forward in prophecy. The Levites were commissioned to praise and prophesy in 1 Chronicles 25, and in 1 Samuel 10 and 19 even stubborn-hearted Saul ended up praising and prophesying when the Holy Spirit came upon him. Likewise, the early disciples were filled with the Spirit and this too was marked by prophecy, speaking in tongues, and even acting as drunk and disorderly

> For me I try to 'book end' my day with focused thought and attention towards God, start and end the day with Jesus not the news or social media. I try to lean into other disciplines such as reading, retreating and replenishing.
>
> (Leon Evans, Lifecentral Church, Further Faster Network)

as Saul or any of the Israelites enjoying God's festival gifts.[41] Pentecost was a jazz gig: spontaneous tongues, preaching, and then healing, miracles and radical living.

Praise takes hold of God's future kingdom and celebrates it in the here and now: heart, soul, mind and strength. It is often associated with those who are persecuted and oppressed. It has been expressed in the most wonderful art and music in Church history. It has characterised the rapid growth of the Pentecostal movement worldwide over the last 100 years. The gift of praise brings with it joy, an energy for life, and a renewed heart that overcomes fear, awkwardness and buttoned-down stoicism. Loving God with all our heart, soul, mind and strength is so healthy!

41. Acts 2:1-21; 19:6-7.

Living Room

Worship in our everyday lives: Cultivating and keeping in the world

> Who may ascend the mountain of the LORD?
> Who may stand in his holy place?
> The one who has clean hands and a pure heart . . .
>
> (Psalm 24:3-4)

Of course, we do not have to literally climb a mountain to worship God, and there are plenty of meetings between people and God in the Bible that are not on mountains. But this is a rich symbolism to help us see that focused devotion, retreat, effort and an expanded sense of vision are all important when we consider how we worship.

Being living sacrifices

The thing about dirty hands and a corrupt heart is that we all know this is a miserable way to live. Sin – selfishness, violence, pride, disobedience – is not just an old-fashioned word that is preached to keep the masses fearfully and guiltily in their place. Sin is real and so totally destructive. We know this when our words and behaviour hurt someone. We feel it when others deceive and wound us. It is seen in newspapers, on film, in gossip columns and in footage of wars, violence and oppression from all over the world. It is not only certain actions that are wrong, it is a spiritual bondage that leads to patterns of behaviour that 'steal . . . kill and destroy' (John 10:10). Discipleship is about living like Jesus in a way that is free from the power of sin and in a way that, marvellously, we are empowered to avoid sin and habitually choose goodness. This is what it means to be a holy people – the desire of God for Israel mentioned many times in Deuteronomy.[42] So how can any of us 'ascend the hill of the Lord' (Psalm 24:3, ESV)? Like us, the Apostle Paul cries out in Romans 7, what a 'wretched man' he is (v. 4) – doing what he doesn't want to do and not doing what he knows is right.

Jesus' act of worship, to give himself as an 'offering' for us (Romans 8:3) so that there is no condemnation and so that we can fulfil righteousness because of being found in him and his purity, shows that worship is the place of freedom, cleansing and holiness. Inspired by the way Jesus offered his life, and in full view of God's mercy, Paul writes in Romans 12 that we too must offer our bodies as living sacrifices, 'holy and pleasing to God' (v. 1). This is true worship! Giving ourselves. And as we do, our hands become clean and our hearts become pure.

A disciple, then, is not one who is conformed to the 'pattern of this world' (v. 2) – self-centred, defensive, avoiding, envious – but transformed by 'renewing [their] mind'. Transformation is the focus of our journey of being a follower, and it begins with humble worship – giving the whole of ourselves to God. This includes our upbringing, personality, ambitions, relationships, family, work, money and desires.

> 'Truly I tell you,' Jesus replied, 'no one who has left home or brothers or sisters or mother or father or children or fields for me and the gospel will fail to receive a hundred times as much in this present age: homes, brothers, sisters, mothers, children and fields – along with persecutions – and in the age to come eternal life. But many who are first will be last, and the last first.'
>
> (Mark 10:29-31)

42. See Deuteronomy 7:6, 14:2,21; 28:9; 33:3.

Whole life, seamless worship

If we are to be seamless, as mentioned earlier, then we specifically want to meet with God and show our love for him in the everyday context in which we find ourselves. One of the words that is used in the Hebrew Bible for worship is *abad,* and it means to work or serve. We see it used of the first humans who were told to 'cultivate' and 'keep' the garden of Eden (Genesis 2:15, NASB1995). The word 'cultivate' is this word *abad.* They were serving the earth, working it and giving themselves to it with devotion and also receiving from it an abundance. The other command given to them here is to 'keep', *shamar.* This means to guard or protect. It is the same word used when Israel is told to keep God's commandments. It does not mean to possess selfishly but instead to honour and revere, and also defend from harm and misuse. The work of the Levites who enable all the worship of the tabernacle is also defined by these two words. To keep (*shamar*) the furnishings and the duties of the tabernacle, and to do or perform (*abad*) the serving there.[43]

> Many ROC[44] volunteers would say it starts with: Prayerful preparation before serving (e.g. Street Angels begin each night with prayer and reflection). Serving regularly – getting out in your community shifts perspective and deepens your awareness of God's presence. Reflecting with others – debriefs, mentor check-ins, and community gatherings help people process, grow, and stay grounded. Those rhythms – serving, praying, reflecting – create space for God's presence in practical, life-giving ways.
>
> (Debra Green, Redeeming Our Communities)

43. Numbers 3:8.
44. https://roc.uk.com/ (accessed 6.11.25).

We are called, like Israel and specifically the Levites, to be 'a kingdom of priests and a holy nation' (Exodus 19:6). This means that the work we *do* and the *care* we take – of people, creation, faith, resources – is the same as the commandments we *keep*, and the worship we *perform* as followers of Jesus.

Jesus works hard in Mark's Gospel, at times missing meals and being surrounded on all sides.[45] This is also his worship and love for God. Jesus cares for people and invites them to touch him for healing.[46] In this he fulfils the law, showing his love for God. This is not just reactive work – where the busier he is the more he is obeying the Great Commandment. Jesus was able to plan how he fulfilled this command in such a way that he was effective, peaceful and free. His work is worship that is freely given, not a compulsive striving. Ken Benjamin works with the London Institute of Contemporary Christianity and has written about whole-life discipleship in his book and set of resources, *Vital Signs*.[47] Ken notes that in Mark 1, when Jesus' ministry is exploding, his disciples urge him to just carry on doing more – if ministry is working, don't stop![48] But Jesus is absolutely committed to a whole-life approach to loving God and people,

> Starting my day with Bible reading and study is important as it enables me to invite God into my day from the beginning. I also try to prayer walk several times a week in my local community, which focuses my prayers on the needs within my community (and keeps them from becoming self-centred or a shopping list).
>
> (Janneke Klos, Count Everyone In)

45. Mark 3:20; 5:24.
46. Mark 6:54-56.
47. Ken Benjamin, *Vital Signs* (London: IVP, 2024).
48. Mark 1:36-39.

and has a plan how to do this well. This kind of lived-out discipleship is not yet another task in the already busy week of the committed churchgoing Christian. It is the heart of how we follow Jesus. We are disciples in our work and in our care, and we can learn to put this into practice in our personal devotional life, at home and at work, and also with others in church. When we see work as worship we are the more able to also enjoy rest as worship, and play as worship, too.

Brother Lawrence was a seventeenth-century monk, and his deep but everyday spirituality is recorded in *The Practice of the Presence of God*.[49] In the section 'The Fourth Conversation' it is written:

> As Brother Lawrence had found such an advantage in walking in the presence of God, it was natural for him to recommend it earnestly to others; but his example was a stronger inducement than any arguments he could propose. His very countenance was edifying, such a sweet and calm devotion appearing in it as could not but affect the beholders. And it was observed that in the *greatest hurry of business in the kitchen he still preserved his recollection and heavenly* mindedness. He was never hasty nor loitering, but did each thing in its season, with an even, uninterrupted composure and tranquillity of spirit. 'The time of business,' said he, 'does not with me differ from the time of prayer, and in the noise and clatter of my kitchen, while several persons are at the same time calling for different things, I possess God in as great tranquillity as if I were upon my knees at the blessed sacrament.'

49. Brother Lawrence, *The Practice of the Presence of God* (New Kensington, PA: Whitaker House, 1982).

Together we are rising/growing into 'a holy temple in the Lord' (Ephesians 2:21), which means that wherever we are can be holy ground and a place to meet face to face with God. Like Brother Lawrence it can be in kitchen duties, or it may be marking students' work, stacking shelves in the supermarket, filling in the spreadsheet, or working the phones.

Therefore our *work* is our *worship* to God.

Our *care* is the way we *keep* his commandments.

Engagement and retreat

In Mark's Gospel we see Jesus engage and retreat. Ched Myers in his commentary on Mark, *Binding the Strong Man*,[50] identifies this rhythm all through the missions of Jesus. There are places of engagement – synagogue, marketplace, temple and desolate places – where there is often conflict and opposition; and places of withdrawal – the mountain, home, seaside, wilderness – where there is safety (even if that keeps getting interrupted!).

In our own lives we can consider where are the places (geographical, social, spiritual) that demand our active engagement. This might be work, household demands,

> Being a disciple in the everyday means living *with* Jesus. Making him the centre of everything, in the exciting and ordinary moments. Letting him shape my thinking, emotions and actions.
>
> (Nicky Wong, All Hallows Church, Bow)

50. Ched Myers, *Binding the Strong Man* (Maryknoll, NY: Orbis Books, 2008).

parenting, school and even church responsibilities. If we only give ourselves to these places of activity – however good and noble that might be – then we will become exhausted. Jesus was incredibly busy caring for people but he kept looking for safe places where he could withdraw and replenish, to be with God and to share spiritual life with his friends. As we saw above, Jesus planned his life well, so that he could live a greater life rather than a lesser one; a life of focus and satisfaction rather than exhaustion and depletion. It does not appear that he felt he was letting people down by sending the crowds off or slipping away to pray. But we know it is easy to feel guilty that we are not doing more for our family, church or workplace – especially when we want to be seen as a good and kind witness to others.

Loving God with all our heart and worshipping him is a gift for us – to be filled with his presence and find our place of security and peace in relationship with God. This rhythm filled Jesus with rest and power to go back and engage in his ministry. Where are the places that are most safe and replenishing for you, and what are the kinds of activity that fill you up with grace and peace? It might be walking in the forest,

> Reading God's Word and allowing it to speak into my very being. Actively praying and inviting the Holy Spirit into my situations and finally being accountable to others, and vice versa. This helps me with my mind and heart, and then practically expressing gratitude, praise, and forgiveness. These daily, simple but powerful practices recalibrate my heart and help keep me walking in step with God.
>
> (Warren Evans, Sports Chaplaincy UK)

in the hills, or by the sea. Or perhaps it's a favourite café? Maybe you have a chair in a room where you often sit and pray easily. Perhaps there is a worship, prayer or study event in church that always does you good – your small group, or a communion service. It might be gardening, DIY, tinkering with the motorbike, going shopping, or sharing a meal with close friends.

For Jesus, these times were often highjacked by crowds following him, or finding his house full of people. The sea sometimes turned on him and became a place of threat rather than gently lapping peace. Nevertheless, Jesus always seeks to withdraw when he can – negotiating any surprises and always kindly responding to those in need – and this shows how highly he valued protecting his heart, soul, mind and strength.

Spiritual pathways

I am a seaside person – I love coastal paths and rockpools. Others I know would prefer the mountains. I also really like sitting with a cup of tea and the Bible in a place where no one can find me. Others I know are often more refreshed by

> When I'm looking after myself well in body, spirit and soul, I find I have more energy, compassion and capacity to serve my family, friends, clients, lead in ministry and be present in my community. When I am serving him I experience him more. It's like being in a 'sweet spot'. Simple daily rhythms like a quiet time first thing, daily muscle work and a daily walk or run, eating well and taking time out to do fun stuff helps me to experience more of him and to listen to him better.
>
> (Gaynor van der Burton, FitFish)

being with people, talking together. We all need people and we all need to be on our own, but there may be some natural spiritual pathways that we find we prefer. John Ortberg and Ruth Hayley Barton, in their book *An Ordinary Day with Jesus*,[51] identify a number of different ways in which we might connect with God and allow our hearts to be filled with his Word and Spirit. Here are their suggestions:

Intellectual – learning draws you close to God. You enjoying thinking, teaching and theology.

Relational – significant relationships cause spiritual growth. You enjoy being with others, talking and doing together.

Serving – helping others bring the presence of God close to you. You enjoy serving others, making a difference, seeing needs fulfilled.

Worship – your heart opens and you come alive in corporate worship times. You enjoy praising God, singing, and listening to others sing in worship.

Activist – purpose and accomplishment align your heart and mind with God's will. You enjoy problem solving, action and making a difference.

Contemplative – solitude and reflection fill your heart. You enjoy silence, stillness, prayer and hearing God's voice.

Creation – responding to God happens when you are surrounded by beauty and awe. You enjoy the outdoors, the art of making and how the physical senses lead you to God.

51. John Ortberg, Ruth Hayley Barton, *An Ordinary Day with Jesus* (Grand Rapids, MI: Zondervan, 2001), pp. 66-90.

These, of course, are not exhaustive and we may find that we answer differently at various times. Nevertheless, an exercise like this (the book mentioned has a questionnaire to follow) helps give us permission to be who we are in God, and worship him 'in Spirit and in truth' (John 4:23-24). It also challenges us to look out for ways of stretching our hearts and minds so that we can love God fully when we are not in our comfort zone.

Spiritual disciplines of the heart

The reality of life is that it tends to squeeze out holiness and our capacity for love. Noise, hurry and crowds characterised Jesus' world and also are typical of our own. All of which make demands on our hearts which then become easily depleted. In the same way that an athlete does not naturally and easily run a marathon without training, so we too need to train in order to be spiritually fit, full and alert.[52] But training

> For me, I feel most alive and most connected to God when taking time in nature; when I'm surrounded by the beauty and diversity of what he has created. I find that when I'm in the presence of waves gently rolling onto the beach that I'm also in the presence of God. That when I walk through the greenery of a forest that the noise of the world slows down and I embrace the time with just myself and him. My most significant prayers, conversations and moments have been when I'm faced with the rivers, trees, beaches and hilltops that can't help but worship Him, simply through their existence.
>
> (Bethan Newman, Youth for Christ)

52. 1 Corinthians 9:24-27.

– enjoyable, fulfilling, impressive as it may be – is a means to an end. Mark's Gospel is full of conflict between those who think holiness is mainly to do with outward behaviour (impressive training regimes) and Jesus, who says it starts in the 'heart' (Mark 7:1-23). Even though holiness affects how we behave, it is not to be measured in outward religious practice. It is measured by God in the hidden place and will be displayed in the 'fruit of the Spirit' (Galatians 5:22-23). Nevertheless, spiritual practices are the way for us to become more like Jesus and to love God with all our heart, soul, mind and strength.

In his book, *Celebration of Discipline*,[53] Richard Foster categorises twelve spiritual disciplines.

Inward disciplines of Meditation, Prayer, Fasting and Study.

Outward disciplines (inward realities resulting in outward lifestyles) in Simplicity, Solitude, Submission and Service.

Corporate disciplines of Confession, Worship, Guidance and Celebration.

> I would describe being a disciple, or follower, of Jesus like on-the-job training – learning directly from the perfect teacher and role model, but also learning from those around me and from my own successes and failures.
>
> (Peter Wilson, Spring Harvest, Physiotherapist)

53. Richard Foster, *Celebration of Discipline* (London: HarperCollins, eBook Reader, 2003).

Examples of inward disciplines

Foster states that meditation is discipline that helps us listen well to God's voice and obey God's word.[54] That's what we all want! Jesus had obviously meditated on Scripture and the Word of God and so knew how to negotiate temptations and pressures in the will of God. Meditation on Scripture is not reading it and forgetting it, but reading it, reflecting on it and allowing it to make sense in and of our own lives. It is worth giving time to the Bible in this way so that the word and mind of God shapes our own thinking. Listening to Lectio 365 is a great way to start this habit. There are devotions to follow morning, noon and night each day. It is a very helpful and rich resource. You can listen to it anytime, anywhere, or read it. What a gift! (The team at 24-7 Prayer have crafted an example of their Lectio 365 for each part of this book, in the Playground section.)

Foster claims that all those we revere who have walked with God have made prayer the main focus of their lives. Prayer is the main way that God transforms us. Like meditation, it takes time but there are so many different ways of praying and listening to God's voice that we will not become tired or bored. A good way to start is to pray when there's nothing else to do. This obviously means avoiding the easy distraction of the phone! But walking the dog, waiting in a GP surgery,

> Being a disciple means having a relationship with Jesus and intentionally inviting him into my day – through prayer, reading (or listening to) the Bible and being in fellowship with others.
>
> (Janneke Klos, Count Everyone In)

54. Ibid, p. 17.

sitting on a bus, even waiting for the microwave to ping are all times where we can pour out our hearts, list the things we are thankful for, and give our imagination to God. What will happen soon enough is that we will find that these slots are not enough – the dog will have to walk for longer, the GP will have to wait, we'll get off at a bus stop miles beyond our destination and the food will go cold. Prayer always becomes more interesting and eagerly demanding the more we do it. Read Pete Greig's *How to Pray*[55] or follow the 24-7 Prayer Course for more help on this.[56]

Dallas Willard in his book, *Spirit of the Disciplines*,[57] outlines a similar list with different but equally helpful categories. He has two classifications.

> **Disciplines of abstinence:** how we might make space for more of God by removing things that distract or, if not checked, corrupt us, through stopping, denying, waiting.
>
> **Disciplines of engagement:** how we might build into our lives activities and habits that strengthen us and enable us to be filled with the Holy Spirit.

Abstinence

Solitude – being away from distractions and learning to know God's love for us.

Silence – no words or sounds so that we can listen to our hearts and God's heart.

Fasting – going without the things that we rely on in our body that influence our soul such as food or media.

Frugality – having less, and being wise with what we do have.

Chastity – self-control and purity in our sexual lives.

55. Pete Greig, *How to Pray* (London: Hodder & Stoughton, 2019).
56. https://prayercourse.org/ (accessed 31.10.25).
57. Dallas Willard, *The Spirit of the Disciplines* (San Francisco, CA: HarperSanFrancisco, 2025).

Secrecy – dealing with our motivations for why we might do things for others to know about.

Sacrifice – giving yourself away.

Engagement

Study – deepening understanding of God through the Bible, theology and resources.

Worship – giving attention to God with reverence, love, praise and devotion.

Celebration – recognising and enjoying the gifts and blessings of God.

Service – using talents and time to serve others and so live a Jesus-style life.

Prayer – talking and listening to God, communing with him for guidance, intercession and thanksgiving.

Fellowship – building and living in relationship with other believers and so expressing the body of Christ.

Confession – acknowledging and turning away from sin and receiving forgiveness.

Submission – surrendering to God's will and living humbly according to his purposes.

For me, journalling has become a spiritual discipline – not just recording what I think or feel, but making space to listen. Asking questions, noting down patterns, and learning to recognise where God is inviting me into greater truth and freedom. Usually I put on some quiet worship, turn my phone off and create time and space for Jesus in my thinking, feeling and being.

(Arianna Walker, Mercy Ministries)

In training to live a greater life

All these lists of disciplines and activities, good habit discoveries that others have made which they now suggest to us all can be overwhelming. Rather than inspiring us to find ways of living that grow a healthy heart, the lack of spiritual activities that we do can make us feel a failure and inadequate. This is not the intention of any of the helpful people who, down the centuries, have found ways to help themselves grow as disciples, especially in their personal relationship with Jesus. You will notice that all these disciplines are mentioned in the Psalms. The Psalms are a handbook of prayer, songs and poems that express the need and desire to live a habitually disciplined life. None of these habits are pursued in order to find salvation or access to the love of God. These are both gifts that are freely given by our heavenly Father. But these gifts are more easily received, held, appreciated and lived in fully when we adopt the disciplines described in the Bible with the aim of living a beloved life.

It is best to see these habits as training. They are ways of training our hearts, souls and minds, and our bodies, to be in a place where we can receive the power and love of the Holy Spirit. It is the Spirit who makes the difference in us and shapes us to be more like Jesus. But like Jesus, when we fast, or pray, or give, or seek some time alone, or join in with worship, we then train ourselves to focus on the Holy Spirit while living on the earth. And this kind of life is well worth living! Being full of the Spirit, being filled with the Spirit, being in the power of the Spirit – wherever we may be – is the way of Jesus. And it works well – in the good times and the challenging times. So, where's a good place to start this personal devotional journey for you?

Up the mountain: A story

There are so many worship moments in the Bible where it feels like heaven breaks onto the earth. Worship really is the invitation into God's presence and the vibrant love that is expressed in the Trinity. When Gideon offers a sacrifice, fire burns it up and says he has seen God 'face to face' (Judges 6:20-24). After Solomon's prayer when the temple is opened, the presence of God comes down in fire and everyone bows down 'to the ground' (2 Chronicles 7:1-3). The room is 'shaken' when the apostles pray (Acts 4:31). I don't experience fire coming down and the room shaking when I worship, but I have often felt an inner fire and a soul shaking, and at times these have even brought with them a physical heat and trembling. There are times when I do feel in my heart that heaven is close to the earth, and I am moved, intrigued, silenced or excited. I remember being away with some others at a gathering that was all about worship. There were musicians and singers there, and the songwriter Graham Kendrick had just done a workshop inviting singers to prophetically improvise around a psalm. So when we all gathered together, we worshipped and sang and the sound was amazing! I turned to the person next to me and said how impressed I was with what he had learned from Graham in that prophetic singing class – as well as being amazed by just about everyone else in the room. But he said it wasn't him singing well at all. As I listened, the sounds were like harmonics and they weren't rising upwards from the congregation but were somehow rushing and streaming over our heads across the high ceiling. Lots of other people heard this, too. It was stunningly beautiful; blending in but quite different from the songs we were singing. I could only conclude – along with others there – that this must have been the sound of angels.

Since then, I have been to that particular place many times. I haven't heard that wonderful sound again, but I have seen people healed extraordinarily, and filled with the Holy Spirit in physically overwhelming, impossible to stand, Solomon-bowing-on-the-pavement ways. It feels a special place, like those mountains of Moses.

But most of my mountain meetings with Jesus are at home, or quietly walking by the canal, or sitting in my church with others, worshipping and praying. The only true response to the love of Jesus is to love him with all our heart, soul, mind and strength – and this is the most wonderful activity under heaven.

Artist: Ruth Hearson

Playground

For all the resources, links and information about the contributors mentioned, scan the code to visit:

www.springharvest.org/resources/no-greater-life/

Practices

For some excellent teaching and resources on living a life like this, take a look at Andrew Roberts' book and course, *Holy Habits*.[58] Andrew covers so many of these disciplines in a very real and accessible way. There are resources for groups and churches, too.

24-7 Prayer has great resources. Along with Lectio 365 mentioned above, you may wish to read *How to Pray* by Pete Greig (mentioned above). They have also designed brilliant courses for groups and churches including The Prayer Course: https://prayercourse.org/ (as previously mentioned).

Explore some practices that help us to become close to Jesus and to be set apart: Worship, prayer, silence, scripture, fasting, repentance, submission, etc.

Resources

Richard Foster, *Celebration of Discipline* (London: Hodder & Stoughton, 2008)

Dallas Willard, *The Spirit of the Disciplines* (San Francisco, CA: HarperSanFrancisco, 2025)

John Ortberg, Ruth Hayley Barton, *An Ordinary Day with Jesus* (Grand Rapids, MI: Zondervan, 2001)

Ruth Hayley Barton, *Sacred Rhythms: Arranging Our Lives for Spiritual Transformation* (Downers Grove, IL: IVP, 2006)

58. www.holyhabits.org.uk/ (accessed 4.11.25).

Donald S. Whitney, *Spiritual Disciplines for the Christian Life* (Carol Stream, IL: Tyndale House Publishers, 2014)

John Mark Comer, *The Ruthless Elimination of Hurry* (London: Hodder & Stoughton, 2019)

Prayer

A breath prayer is a simple, short prayer said in a single breath. You pray the first line slowly breathing in, and the second line slowly breathing out.

> Lord God, fill me with your Holy Spirit.
> I receive your love,
> and release my insecurity.
> I receive your joy,
> and release my unhappiness.
> I receive your peace,
> and release my anxiety.
> I receive your patience,
> and release my impulsiveness . . .[59]

You can write a breath prayer around any scripture.

> I've found it an incredibly helpful practice in times of busyness or stress as it can be prayed while working, walking, or during a short break. (Sheridan Voysey)

Lectio Divina 2

The Heaviness of God
2 Chronicles 7:1–3

59. You can find the full prayer at www.sheridanvoysey.com/breathprayer (accessed 31.10.25).

Let's pause and pray with a *Lectio 365* Morning Prayer, meditating on the moment when the glory of God descended on the temple.

Together we will pray (P.R.A.Y.): P – pausing to be still, R – rejoicing with a psalm and reflecting on Scripture, A – asking God to help us and others, and Y – yielding to his will in our lives.

Pause

As I enter prayer now, I pause to be still; to breathe slowly, to re-centre my scattered senses upon the presence of God.

Pause and pray

Prayer of Approach

Great and glorious King, I draw near to you today.
Awaken my heart to behold you, show me your glory.
Let me grow in wonder of who you are, show me your glory.
May gratitude overflow for all that you do, show me your glory.
Remind me of your presence throughout this day, show me your glory.

Rejoice and reflect

I choose to rejoice in God's joy-giving presence today, joining with the ancient praise of all God's people in the words of Psalm 16:

> No wonder my heart is glad, and I rejoice.
> My body rests in safety.
> For you will not leave my soul among the dead
> or allow your holy one to rot in the grave.
> You will show me the way of life,
> granting me the joy of your presence
> and the pleasures of living with you forever.
>
> (Psalm 16:9-11, NLT)

Pause and pray

King Solomon has fulfilled his Father's dream of building a temple for God. I reflect on the moment God's glory descended on that special place, in response to Solomon's prayer . . .

> When Solomon finished praying, fire came down from heaven and consumed the burnt offering and the sacrifices, and the glory of the LORD filled the temple. The priests could not enter the temple of the LORD because the glory of the LORD filled it. When all the Israelites saw the fire coming down and the glory of the LORD above the temple, they knelt on the pavement with their faces to the ground, and they worshipped and gave thanks to the LORD, saying,
>
> 'He is good;
> his love endures for ever.'
>
> (2 Chronicles 7:1-3)

God comes to dwell in the temple; his presence is so thick and heavy that people can't enter it! The Hebrew word for 'glory' (*kabod*) finds its root in the Hebrew word for 'heavy' (*kabed*). God is not a lightweight God, yet I live in a society that treats God lightly. It's easy to say 'I believe in God' yet he carries no weight in my life. God is not ethereal, out there somewhere floating around meaning very little. He is in fact present, real, and the heaviness of his glory can dwell in me.

Ask

Imagine if God's presence was so heavy in my life that nothing else could get in!

Lord, help me not to treat you as a lightweight God. Come and have full access in my life today. Fill me, Lord, cleanse me, and may my life be full of you.

Pause and pray

Lord, would you come and dwell in my community? As you filled Solomon's temple, would you fill your living temple, the Church? May my church represent you well to the world around us. May we reveal you in such a glorious way to others that they can't help but acknowledge your greatness and worship you.

Pause and pray

Yield

As I return to today's passage, I listen for a word or phrase that speaks particularly into my personal context today.

> When Solomon finished praying, fire came down from heaven and consumed the burnt offering and the sacrifices, and the glory of the Lord filled the temple. The priests could not enter the temple of the LORD because the glory of the LORD filled it. When all the Israelites saw the fire coming down and the glory of the LORD above the temple, they knelt on the pavement with their faces to the ground, and they worshipped and gave thanks to the LORD, saying,
>
> 'He is good;
> his love endures for ever.'
>
> (2 Chronicles 7:1-3)

What is the particular invitation of the Holy Spirit to me today through this passage?

Pause

I notice the response of the people. When the fire of God's presence arrived and the people witnessed the glory of the Lord fill the temple, all they could do was fall down and say, 'He is good; his love endures for ever.'

God's glory elicits a response; when God is present, I worship.

Pause and pray

Yielding Prayer

Lord, I yield to you today by repeating the prayer from today's passage:

> You are good and your love endures for ever.

Yielding Promise

And now, as I prepare to take this time of prayer into the coming day, the Lord who loves me says in the Psalms:

> Great are the works of the Lord;
> they are pondered by all who delight in them.
> Glorious and majestic are his deeds,
> and his righteousness endures for ever.
>
> (Psalm 111:2-3)

Closing prayer

Father, help me to live this day to the full,
being true to you in every way.
Jesus, help me to give myself away to others,
being kind to everyone I meet.
Spirit, help me to love the lost,
proclaiming Christ in all I do and say.
Amen.

Lectio 365 is a prayer app from 24-7 Prayer. Download for free to pray the Bible morning, noon and night.

Further Bible verses to read and reflect on

Exodus 34:4-5; 2 Chronicles 6:40 – 7:3

Worship

Brother Lawrence is well known for experiencing the presence of God when peeling potatoes. In what everyday activity, chore or time could you turn your heart towards Jesus and actively worship him. Set time aside to try this!

Journal – pray, reflect, write

Consider your own rhythms of engagement and withdrawal.

Where and how are you finding the presence of God when you are engaged – with people, at work, with church, in household life? In what ways are you filled and in what ways are you depleted?

....

....

....

What does withdrawal look like for you? Is it a slower pace, a different place, on your own, with close friends, in life-giving activities?

....

....

....

How do you manage interruptions?

....

....

....

....

What are the rhythms of the day, week, month or year that the Holy Spirit is calling you into?

....

....

....

....

Action

Plan a creative worship event or space that calls disciples and/or those without faith into God's presence.

- This could be outside.
- What about a space in your house?
- You may wish to explore a hospital or airport chapel/prayer-room
- Look at Prayer Spaces in Schools: https://prayerspacesinschools.com/

Find out more about Presence Revival and worship on the streets: https://presencerevival.com/

Group Bible study

A tale of two worship times

Mark 9:2-13 and Mark 14:1-10

- Why does Jesus take Peter, James and John up the mountain with him?
- What happened to each of Moses and Elijah last time they were on mountains? And what therefore could happen with Peter, James and John?
- Why might Peter want to package this precious moment?
- The transfiguration leads to the voice of God.[60] Talk together about experiencing and hearing God.
- Compare this high-mountain story with the woman at the hilltop village of Bethany.
- Who were the people being indignant and rebuking harshly the woman who was worshipping Jesus?[61]
- Compare her generous and immediate act of devotion with Peter's plan for worship.
- Compare Peter not knowing what to say in 9:6 with the woman's direct and prophetic action in 14:8.
- How understandable are Peter's reaction and the people's reaction to the woman, and why are both dismissed by God and Jesus?
- Pray for one another, for hearts of devotion, humility and listening so that in the coming days you will each hear from the Holy Spirit as you worship.

60. See also Exodus 34:29-35; 1 Kings 19:11-13; Daniel 10:2-12.
61. See also Matthew 26:8-10.

Wholehearted – a series of studies about the heart #2

In 1 Chronicles 28:9 David says to Solomon:

> And you, my son Solomon, acknowledge the God of your father, and serve him with wholehearted devotion and with a willing mind, for the LORD searches every heart and understands every desire and every thought.

Notice wholeheartedness and a willing mind (literally soul) are bound together again, as they are in the Great Commandment. Solomon is to be someone who delights in serving and to be one who is fully whole and at peace in his love for God. David also says here that it is God himself who searches the heart and understands fully how our clever, plotting and devising minds can be – for good or for ill! Read also Psalm 139.

Have you noticed the phrase of Jesus to the Pharisees in Luke's version of the story when the man was lowered through the roof?

> The Pharisees and the teachers of the law began thinking to themselves, 'Who is this fellow who speaks blasphemy? Who can forgive sins but God alone?'

> Jesus knew what they were thinking and asked, 'Why are you *thinking these things in your hearts*?
>
> (Luke 5:21-22, my emphasis)

Jesus is showing that he knows what people are thinking, just like Yahweh in 1 Chronicles. But how interesting that Luke uses the phrase: 'He knew what they were *thinking in their hearts*' (my emphasis). Although we tend to centre our thoughts in our heads and our emotions in our hearts, we probably all understand this phrase that identifies a deep kind of thinking that takes place within us, often from our old selves but hopefully from our new identity in Christ, which drives and motivates our behaviours.

The Heartstyles Indicator is a coaching tool devised by corporate consultant Stephen Klemich and clinical psychologist Dr Mara Klemich.[62] It is a tool that has been used in business settings to help individuals and teams identify their heart behaviours.

In their model, they have an illustration with four quadrants. Above a central horizontal line, two quadrants of humility and love, and below that horizontal line two quadrants of pride and fear.

The team identified typical human heart behaviours that are 'Below the line'.

'Sarcastic', 'Competitive', 'Controlling' and 'Striving' – all which stem from a self-promoting place of pride;

62. https://heartstyles.com/book (accessed 1.11.25).

'Approval seeking', 'Easily offended', 'Dependent' and 'Avoiding' – all of which stem from a self-protecting place of fear.

They also identified heart behaviours that are 'above the line':

'Authentic', 'Transforming', 'Reliable' and 'Achieving' – all of which stem from a place of humility where we desire our own personal growth;

'Relating', 'Encouraging', 'Developing' and 'Compassionate' – all of which stem from a place of love where we desire to grow others.

Do you recognise any of these below or above the line behaviours in yourself?

Do you recognise any of these behaviours in the Bible?

Before they embarked on this huge project of data collection and research, this is where the Klemich's found these heart behaviours: in the Bible.

In Genesis 3, Adam and Eve decided to put themselves in the place of God, desiring his position of ultimate judgement. That was pride. Adam blamed God and the woman for what had happened. Eve said she had been deceived. Both of them were hiding from God and each other and became afraid. From then on there were behaviours such as striving, controlling, approval seeking and denial.

In Philippians 2 and 1 John 3 we read that Jesus, who is God, humbled himself to become a human, being obedient to death on a cross; this is how we know what love is. The good news of the Gospel is that God has given us new hearts, the heart of Jesus, so that we can learn to love like him and live humbly like him. We can renew our minds and have cleansed and sincere hearts. We can live above the line.

Questions

Read Genesis 3:6-13. What do you notice in this passage about behaviours of pride and fear?

Sarcasm can be funny. In what ways do we use humour to put others down or elevate ourselves? Do you like people being sarcastic to or about you?

Competition can be healthy. However, in what ways is a competitive spirit destructive – to yourself or to others, and why?

What situations for people do you tend to avoid, and why? What do you put off even though it is important?

It is often rewarding to be praised and recognised. Why do we often overly seek approval from others, and in what ways or situations do we get easily offended?

Read 1 Corinthians 13:4-8a. How does love deal with these issues we have just been talking about?

We need an encounter with Jesus to truly change our hearts and deliver us from old patterns of behaviour – for instance, Zacchaeus in Jericho in Luke 19:1-10, Saul near Damascus in Acts 9:1-22, Peter in Joppa in Acts 11:1-18. Pray (for one another if you are in a group) to meet with Jesus in significant ways.

Artist: Lynne Pugh

I saw myself wandering on a mountainside following first one path and then another. As I neared the top, I heard the voice of Jesus say, 'Come to me, follow me.' On a rock sat Jesus. I sat next to him and he put his arm around me and said, 'I've got this! You don't need to keep seeking "the way" from others, just trust me.'

Proverbs 3:5: 'Trust in the Lord with all your heart and lean not on your own understanding; in all your ways submit to him, and he will make your paths straight.'

(Lynne Pugh)

PART THREE

In The House

Looking in:
to love Jesus and one another
in Christ-centred communities

Classroom

God is Love. For love to be truly expressed and received, there has to be relationship. The theology of the Trinity has been robustly developed by Church fathers and theologians down the ages and is being dynamically explored in contemporary scholarship. One of the words used to describe the nature of the Trinity is perichoresis.[63] It is the mutual indwelling, cohering and interpenetrating within the Godhead. This is that

> God as three in one is one of the great mysteries of the Christian faith in that it's hard for us to imagine one thing that is also three but this is the revelation of God we're given. All the pictures we use to describe the Trinity fall short in some way of really telling us that God is one essence and three persons who are all one. Father, Son, and Holy Spirit are distinct from one another and relate to one another in perfect love and unity but fully share a mind, a will, a nature, authority, majesty, glory, etc. The triune God is a gift to us in that first it tells us that God relates (to himself) and second it tells us how God relates to us, as Father, Son, and Holy Spirit. Coming to one person of the Trinity is coming to all. Praying to one is praying to all. Relating to one is relating to all. And yet we are given different aspects of God's being to speak to and come into relationship to ourselves, Father, Son, and Holy Spirit. He is personal, relational, and takes us up into his own relationship as God in himself, by the Spirit, as sons and children in the Son of our loving heavenly Father. God's greatest gift to humanity.
>
> (Lucy Peppiatt, Theologian and Author, President WTC Theology)

63. It is traditionally understood that this term was first used by Gregory Nazianzen in the fourth century AD and developed by Maximus the Confessor in the seventh century AD.

the three persons of the Trinity share the same space and are inseparable from one another – 'each are in each, and all in each, and each in all, and all are one' as Augustine describes it.[64] Some commentators describe this being like a dance (it is very similar to the word *choreuo*, meaning 'to dance'), and therefore the persons of the Trinity are in communion with each other in a somewhat more individualistic way. In the light of contemporary culture and its emphasis on personhood, identity, individual human rights and relationships, viewing the Trinity as a dance-like Godhead relationship has become a popular view. However, we tend to think of the word 'person' meaning an individual, which in our minds may reduce the Trinity to three people who all get on jolly well. On the other hand, we can also slip into a habit of seeing God as a monolithic and impassive block of power who is hard to approach and who we'll never really relate to. God is neither a collection of separate parts, nor one big lump. Nor is he subject himself to a dance that is bigger than he is. Instead, he is a mystery of loving relationships which co-inhere, make room, indwell, and whose movement causes the movement of all living things. Father, Son and Holy Spirit truly love – from which everything in his creation is breathed into for a dancing and loving life. Whether or not our viewpoint on the mystery

> Discipleship in everyday life is embodying God's will. Jesus redefined our understanding of family by stating, 'Whoever does God's will is my brother and sister and mother' (Mark 3:35), connecting spiritual purpose and our view of family through pursuing deeper intimacy with God.
>
> (Alan Charter, Children Everywhere Walking With Jesus)

64. Augustine, *On the Trinity* (McLean, VA: Beloved Publishing LLC, 2014), 6:10.

of the Godhead is rather too human a perspective, or rather too distant and unknowing, the resurgence in thinking and application of God as love and somehow in loving relationships within 'God-self' enables us to appreciate God's care for creation, and God's openness to loving and being loved by humanity.[65]

Love is real and not just an idea. Jesus is beloved of the Father, and the Holy Spirit brings each of us into a father-child relationship too, which is remarkable![66] Thinking about the Trinity also helps us consider how the Spirit-filled church may, too, reflect God's own experience of love. It is a doctrine that certainly makes sense when reading the story of God and people in the Bible. We see how people become formed by God into a community, where family is both the means and the end: God the Father, Son and Spirit sharing their love here on the earth with those who are now brothers and sisters together, the children of God.

Family is the picture that we are given in Genesis of what God is looking for and how he will redeem the world. He says to Abraham, 'In you all the families of the earth shall be blessed' (Gen 12:3; 28:14, ESV). This is not necessarily a mum, dad and two kids arrangement. It is wide and broad, sometimes messy, with relatives and friends, old and young. It is groups of warriors and pairs of widows. These families mix and match, break and mend. But the picture is of shared life, identity and purpose – a 'family' that is learning to love one another through difference, competition, weakness and estrangement. Jesus himself is born into a family that has its doubts and fears and even wants to disown him at times. He also discovers in

65. For two interesting essays written from opposite perspectives on this doctrine, see Karen Kilby https://onlinelibrary.wiley.com/doi/10.1111/j.1741-2005.2000.tb06456.x (accessed 1.11.25).
and Gregory Gorsuch, www.researchgate.net/publication/373726981_Perichoresis_and_Projection_A_Response_to_Kilby's_Trinitarian_Minimalism (accessed 1.11.25).
66. Mark 1:11; 9:7; Romans 8:15; Galatians 4:6.

his humanity that he is forced to experience separation from God – having to trust that the Father still loves him when he is so alone on the cross.

The love that Jesus experiences from the Father is known in his humanity and not only as the eternal Son. At Jesus' baptism, the voice of the Father is heard saying that Jesus is his beloved, his 'chosen' one (Matt 12:18, Mark 9:7, Luke 9:35), and again at his transfiguration, in Matthew 17:5. It is worth noting that even with this Shema emphasis on loving others – our neighbours in the family of God and in the wider world – it does not mean that this is done at the expense of knowing how loved we are individually by God, and therefore

As a Christian, a disabled person and wheelchair user, I have experienced both challenges and opportunities in each of these areas. The challenges have included physical access difficulties, barriers in attitude and assumptions around my capability and calling (from others and also myself). On the journey I am learning greater reliance on the presence and person of Jesus. I have seen God inter-weave my weakness with His strength. I have known the joy and opportunity of working interdependently together in community with others at Through the Roof and my local church and, whether that's travelling through Tanzania and Kenya to meet local disabled people and pastors (being physically carried over rocks to get there), facilitating training and events or meeting people to pray and encourage one another, one thing is clear – for the whole body of Christ to function – we need each other and when we work together – it's beautiful.

(Kate Budd, Interactive – Disability Equality in Sport)

how we are able to truly love ourselves. There is of course the call to deny ourselves and imitate Jesus in being poured out in service and worship, but this is different to self-loathing or low self-worth. We can give away with such generosity precisely because there is no end to the love that is poured into our hearts by the Holy Spirit. Knowing the love of God for us personally is the heart of the gospel of Jesus. We are beloved children, who call God '*Abba*'! 'See what great love the Father has lavished on us, that we should be called children of God! And that is what we are!' (1 John 3:1). We avoid experiencing this if we can only get our worth from trying hard to love others rather than knowing we are loved and are of such high worth. Jesus truly was able to love his neighbour as he loved himself, because he knew how much he was loved. What good news this is, that the love of God shared eternally in the Trinity, has now broken out into the world through Jesus, and is ours personally, ours to share with God, and ours to share with those around us!

It was Jesus' deep belief in the love he continues to have between Father, Son and Spirit that then led to an outpouring of love on the day of Pentecost. Abraham's blessing comes true and a new family is made out of many tribes and tongues of the earth. In this big story of the Bible, from Genesis to Revelation, we see that God is forming a family who will love him and one another, and also those around them. This shaping of family is seen most clearly with the people of Israel in the wilderness.

Looking in, with God's Deuteronomy People

Deuteronomy is Moses' summing up of the history of the formation of Israel in the wilderness, and a handbook for how to live well with God and one another.

God's purpose is seen in Deuteronomy 7:6: 'For you are a people holy to the LORD your God. The LORD your God has chosen you out of all the peoples on the face of the earth to be his people, his treasured possession.'

To be holy is to be set apart, to be different, to be defined by God's ways and not our own. And to be set apart for Israel is so that they can learn a new way of living and then demonstrate that to others around. Ultimately it is being set apart to love one another. And what an ask that is! Israel really did need the sanctifying work of the Holy Spirit if they were to demonstrate a loving community to a watching world. Their Exodus journey is full of selfishness, moaning, rebellion and distress. They had to learn to share, forgive, prefer, serve; to take the lowest place and the last seat; to trust in God and not rely on their own understanding;[67] to overcome evil by doing good. They were formed into this new people by being washed – literally through the Red Sea and then the Jordan – but spiritually and socially in their sanctification. This was the process of their discipleship, where they had to learn God's ways of relating to

> Applying God's commandments to Israel today demands reflection and clarity about who we are as God's people today, and how a distinctive Christian community represents the kingdom of God in our own culture. Whatever the complexity, there is also consistency – we are still God's treasured possession, and we are always called to live in unity, holiness and purpose together, giving glory to God and hope to the world.
>
> (Cathy Madavan, Speaker and Author)

67. Proverbs 3:5.

one another, rather than the ways they had learned in Egypt of anger, competition and resentment.

This forming is not just so that Israel can get its act together, but also so that the nations around can look and see Israel as a great example of how to live.

> See, I have taught you decrees and laws as the LORD my God commanded me, so that you may follow them in the land you are entering to take possession of it. Observe them carefully, for this will show your wisdom and understanding to the nations, who will hear about all these decrees and say, 'Surely this great nation is a wise and understanding people.' What other nation is so great as to have their gods near them the way the LORD our God is near us whenever we pray to him? And what other nation is so great as to have such righteous decrees and laws as this body of laws I am setting before you today?
>
> Only be careful, and watch yourselves closely so that you do not forget the things your eyes have seen or let them fade from your heart as long as you live. Teach them to your children and to their children after them.
>
> (Deuteronomy 4:5-9)

Emotionally healthy spirituality means a life built on Jesus, allowing him to gently give us a right perspective on ourselves and the world around us. It calls us into a deepening knowledge that we are simply children of a loving heavenly Father, fully known and freely forgiven. In response to that knowledge we are enabled to live abundantly and generously, hearing his voice, following his lead, serving his people and refreshed and empowered by his Spirit.

(Ali Herbert, Gas Street Church)

The laws of Moses are not so that he can have an easy life, presiding over a smooth running but miserable, resentfully law-abiding nation. This teaching is a gift so that Israel's wisdom and understanding will be envied by those around. They are told to 'carefully observe them with all your heart and with all your soul' (Deuteronomy 26:16). When laws make it into our hearts and then are lived from our hearts, then they become ethos and a culture is formed. Forming a new, enjoyable and godly culture was the purpose of the journey and laws in the desert. The Ten Commandments are not simply laws to follow – trying to get through the day without murdering someone is not that hard for most of us. They are also a set of values that describe a new worldview for the Israelite people, which honours people, parents, possessions; and makes room for God's presence, guards against idolatry, putting emphasis on rest and protection in God rather than establishing our own wealth and security.

In his book *An Unstoppable Force*, church and thought leader Erwin McManus comments on the power of influence and identity when laws become ethos. He says that we are told to clean our teeth for a few years – law – but when we are grown we no longer have anyone standing over us each morning forcing this to happen. We do it because we know it is good, we want to. Similarly, we all put our seatbelts on in the car – not because we think we'll get caught by a police officer at the end of the drive, but because we are aware of road safety and do this automatically without begrudging.[68] The ban on smoking in public places in Europe is now celebrated by smoke-smell-free clothes at the end of an evening but more importantly is mostly enforced by the general awareness of risks; to those smoking and to those inhaling around them. McManus says that the beliefs, values and worldviews that

68. Erwin McManus, *An Unstoppable Force* (Colorado Springs, CO: David C. Cook), pp. 99-102.

shape ethos are far more powerful than laws. But if ethos is neglected then rules are all that is left and we become legalistic. He comments that the Church after Pentecost was shaped by a one heart and mind ethos which made far more impact than rule-based religion and eventually turned the Roman Empire upside down.

The power of culture is more influential than laws, even though laws certainly play their part in forming that culture and retaining it. The laws in Deuteronomy helped establish individual habits but also ways of living that were good for the community and which formed rituals and shared practices to strengthen the God-given ethos of justice, righteousness, faithfulness and love. 'Righteousness and justice are the foundation of your throne; love and faithfulness go before you' (Psalm 89:14). These practices meant that the new Israelite community was more physically healthy, able to deal with local tensions and politics, and had robust systems of justice and social equity. Building a 'parapet around your roof' so people don't fall off and injure themselves is good health and safety (Deuteronomy 22:8). Making sure that poorer people can have a go at reaping from your land after you have done your work enables everyone to take part in social care.[69] And being honest with your weighing scales means that your customers will get a fair deal when they come to you.[70] These are practical laws that all have an ethos of justice, kindness and love behind them. They enable a healthy community to be formed. This is what it means to be holy; not being religious or pious, but honouring God's own holiness because the way he loves is through purity and justice. How interesting that the chapter where we find the verse 'Love your neighbour as yourself' (Leviticus 19:18), which is full of commands like the ones we have just referred to in Deuteronomy, begins with

69. Deuteronomy 24:19.
70. Deuteronomy 25:15.

the declaration: 'Be holy because I, the LORD your God, am holy' (v. 1). So holiness is the foundation of a great ethos and leads to a culture of good and right living. The peoples around Israel were not so well formed and so were able to watch and learn – to see good practice in action. This is the way that ethos spreads. A community lives well together so others can experience it, enjoy it, then copy it in order to live in its fruitfulness.

Good community – whether it was the families that God established in Genesis, the people in the wilderness, or then the kingdom of Israel under the valiant and wise rule of people like David and Solomon (unfortunately all these examples often fell spectacularly short of great community) – is the vehicle by which God will bring in his heavenly kingdom of 'righteousness, peace and joy' (Romans 14:17). For Jesus, and then Paul and the apostles, this new community, the Church, plays a similar role to Israel. But this time, the laws are to be written on the people's hearts, not tablets of stone, and are laws of the Holy Spirit, not Moses. The Church was to practise the law of love – loving one another so that others around would know that we are Jesus' disciples.

> Genesis 2:18 reminds us that we were created for community and for cooperation – as John Wesley once said, 'The Bible knows nothing of solitary religion.'[71] It's in community that we grapple with faith and life, discovering how to listen, learn and love well.
>
> (Matt and Amy Summerfield, Zeo Church Hitchin, Reboot Your Leadership, Kyria, Skylark International)

71. https://wesley.nnu.edu/john-wesley/john-wesley-the-methodist/chapter-ix-society-and-class/ (accessed 6.11.25).

This is now the role of the Church. It is a community where we can put into practice the ethos of Jesus and as we do that, develop a culture that is wholesome and attractive to others. It is about serving one another. The Jerusalem church in Acts 6 established a welfare culture. We can do the same – rather than expecting social services to do everything or other people's relatives to carry the burden, we can care for one another as a church, young and old. We can establish a culture of forgiveness and patience. This is where we practise tolerance, loving and listening even when there is difference of opinion or approach. The rhythms and routines of church – even if they are at times too busy and programmed – can challenge us to truly play our part in this mini Jesus society. The cost of such belonging is also its reward.

The blessed life

Practising the law of love is often called 'blessing' in the Bible. Deuteronomy 28 is an extraordinary blessing from God. Living in God's world, God's way, by obeying his commands and putting them into practice, leads to the good life. God's desire is that people will live well together, that the inward dimension of love will attract and enjoy the favour of God.

> All these blessings will come on you and accompany you if you obey the LORD your God:
> You will be blessed in the city and blessed in the country.
> The fruit of your womb will be blessed, and the crops of your land and the young of your livestock – the calves of your herds and the lambs of your flocks.
> Your basket and your kneading trough will be blessed.
> You will be blessed when you come in and blessed when you go out.
>
> (Deuteronomy 28:2-6)

In a similar way, Jesus preaches the law of love for God and each other in the Sermon on the Mount in Matthew 5 – 7. Like Moses, Jesus talks about the blessed life. But rather than the idea of being blessed meaning we have to have lots of money, or avoid disaster, or have no problems, being blessed is the gift of a state of heart and mind in whatever circumstances we find ourselves. It is when the law of God's love that is now written on our hearts causes us to hunger and thirst for righteousness, to be merciful, to make peace. It is when we are humble, even poor in spirit, persecuted, or in mourning. It is when we are pure in heart; reliant on, and a channel for, the grace of God. Jesus pronounces the blessing of God in these circumstances which can actually feel the opposite of what we consider to be the good life. Nevertheless, these blessings are: living in the kingdom of heaven, receiving comfort, inheriting the earth, experiencing satisfaction, being given mercy, seeing God like Moses did, being God's children. This is experienced, not so

> As the CEO of Mercy UK, I've had the privilege of developing and delivering discipleship resources for thousands of people across the UK and beyond. Keys to Freedom has been especially transformational – not just for those we serve, but for our own team and even for me personally, even though I wrote most of it! It's a powerful tool that helps individuals identify lies they've believed, renew their minds with truth, and walk in lasting freedom as disciples of Jesus in the everyday. It's set up as a personal devotional – twenty minutes a day with a pen, a Bible and the Holy Spirit, to deepen our relationship with God, self and others and learn to live free and stay free.
>
> (Arianna Walker, Mercy Ministries)

much by each of us as an individual, but in how we relate and orientate our heart towards others.

The blessing that Jesus promises gives the same results as the blessing that Moses promises – joy, peace and satisfaction – here in our earthly lives. Jesus is insistent that his own teaching is not to abolish the law of Moses, but to fulfil it: to fill it to the brim with meaning and power and to complete it for every situation and circumstance. Jesus references Moses' laws such as do not murder or commit adultery. He also mentions an eye for an eye, and comments on prayer, fasting and giving.[72] According to Jesus, all these laws of Moses are good, but they require a whole life application – heart, soul, mind and strength. And when we give our hearts to these good commands, knowing the ethos behind them and the good nature of the lawgiver, we are then blessed, whatever the circumstances. Because these laws are mostly about how we live with one another in the light of living well with God, then those around us are blessed too.[73]

> To me, emotionally healthy spirituality is the integration of spiritual maturity with emotional wholeness – allowing the Holy Spirit to shape not just our behaviour but our beliefs, our inner life, and how we relate to others. It's where discipleship reaches beyond just surface habits into the hidden places of the heart, bringing freedom, healing, and integrity to the whole person.
>
> (Arianna Walker, Mercy Ministries)

72. Matthew 5:38; 6:1-18.
73. Listen to The Bible Project's episode on the beatitudes for more on 'The Good Life' https://bibleproject.com/podcast/why-do-beatitudes-matter-overworked-and-hopeless/ (accessed 3.11.25).

The place where true community happens

In the last section on Looking Up we saw how God determines the place where his people will gather for worship. Some scholars have seen this as a blueprint for a Jerusalem-centred Israel, a nation where there would be one special place for everyone to come to and recognise one another as family. They see this fulfilled in 2 Chronicles 34 and 35 under the reign of Josiah where the temple is central to everything. Chris Wright, in his commentary on Deuteronomy, argues that God is not forming one big national worship programme.[74] A specific place is never mentioned. Instead, Deuteronomy is about how community is formed around wholehearted love for God, wherever the people are:

> But you are to seek the place the Lord your God will choose from among all your tribes to put his Name there for his dwelling. To that place you must go . . .
>
> (Deuteronomy 12:5)

> I've been blessed enough to walk alongside worship leaders like Graham Kendrick who have always modelled humility and a true love of God to me. 'Keep the main thing the main thing' is something I learned on tour with Uncle G. Thankfully there are many church leaders and ministers I know who have helped shepherd me from a distance too, helping keep my eyes on Jesus. Accountability and true friendship are like gold.
>
> (Philippa Hanna, Singer Songwriter)

74. Christopher Wright, *New International Bible Commentary: Deuteronomy* (Carlisle: Send the Light, 1996), pp. 169-170.

This 'Name' means the identity of his family, his children and their nature, ethos and culture.

'The place where the Lord chooses' (mentioned seventeen times in the book, remember) is wherever people gather to love God with all their heart, soul and strength. In chapter 12, this gathering is characterised by social inclusivity, rejoicing and eating:

> And there rejoice before the Lord your God – you, your sons and daughters, your male and female servants, and the Levites from your towns who have no land allotted to them or any inheritance of their own.
>
> (Deuteronomy 12:12)

Notice that the ethos is one of joy and one of togetherness – ages, social status, dependents. The people are told they must eat together, a lot! Grain, oil, wine and meat. In chapter 12 people are told to eat together rather than on their own, to feast, and to even eat as much as they want! Being together across social divides, rejoicing and eating sounds like the final scene of a great Christmas movie, where forgiveness and friendship are celebrated and competition and insecurity are put away with. This kind of scene is a longing in every human heart. This is the precursor to the family of Jesus in Mark 3:34-35 when he is in a crowded house. Whoever does God's will is his mother, sister, brother. It foreshadows the early Church of Acts 2 and 4 where they freely give and there is no one in need. Widows, orphans and foreigners are also included – not simply as those who will receive fair justice or a welfare handout – but fully included in the community of worship and love.

> And rejoice before the Lord your God at the place he will choose as a dwelling for his Name – you, your sons and daughters, your male and female servants, the Levites in

> your towns, and the foreigners, the fatherless and the widows living among you. Remember that you were slaves in Egypt, and follow carefully these decrees.
>
> (Deuteronomy 16:11-12)

John sums up this Deuteronomy community ethos in his first letter, where he calls church members brothers and sisters, to show that they are new kind of family:

> Whoever claims to love God yet hates a brother or sister is a liar. For whoever does not love their brother and sister, whom they have seen, cannot love God, whom they have not seen. And he has given us this command: anyone who loves God must also love their brother and sister.
>
> (1 John 4:20-21)

This is our calling, too, as the Church that bears the name of Jesus Christ.

> To be washed clean from selfishness and insecurity.
>
> To work together with the Holy Spirit to form a new culture of holiness and oneness.
>
> This is wholehearted love in action.

Access, Belonging, and Commission are the ABC at the heart of following Jesus. *Access* to the Gospel and community, *Belonging* to God and each other, and *Commission* to use our gifts for His glory. As a disabled person, I've faced physical barriers and doubts about my abilities. But I've learned to lean on Jesus' strength and discovered the joy of working interdependently with others. Together, our unique strengths and weaknesses come together for God's glory and the advancement of his kingdom.

(Katie Budd, Interactive – Disability Equality in Sport)

Looking in, with the new community in Mark's Gospel

At home

We saw the initial formation of the apostles up a mountain, where there was a focus on Jesus, on being together and being sent out. Mark highlights the togetherness of this newly formed community throughout his Gospel, often by watching what they do when they are gathered in the house or pausing on their journey.

There are a couple of related words for house in the Greek New Testament – *oikos* and *oikia*. These are generally interchangeable although it could be said that *oikos* may refer more to the building or the household's outward influence and *oikia* may refer more intimately to the interior culture of the home that lives there. Sometimes our Bibles translate it as 'home', sometimes 'house' and sometimes uses the word 'household'. In Mark's Gospel, Jesus is often found in a house or his own home and it is in these places that conversations happen, healing take place and relationship are built.

Jesus is invited to Peter and Andrew's house with James and John, for what we would recognise as after-church-Sunday-lunch (after synagogue on a Saturday . . .) in Mark 1:29-34. Peter's mother-in-law is healed and then she serves them with

> Being a fluid family and opening our home to adoption and fostering has taught us much of the impact of radical hospitality and the need for sensitivity and inclusive approaches in ministry.
>
> (Alan Charter, Children Everywhere Walking With Jesus)

a meal until the place gets packed with loads of people. Their intimacy, eating together, and then managing the needs of others must have built their bonds of friendship enormously and led to this being a particularly tight-knit friendship group within the disciples.

He comes back to Capernaum in chapter 2 and seems to have his own house now. Once again it is packed out with people, including knowledgeable scribes, who are all listening to his teaching. This is a place of learning together – which then gets half destroyed by the four friends of a paralysed man. But cynical hearts are revealed, the man's heart is forgiven, his body is healed and everyone glorifies God. Being in community together around Jesus is good for the mind, the heart, the body and the soul.

He's next seen in his house eating once more! It's Deuteronomy all over again! The way Mark writes this in 2:15-17 shows that it is not a one-off occasion but it is happening all the time. Jesus

> My most effective practices include reading the Bible in a year every year – highlighting verses that catch my attention. A slower daily reading of Scripture reflecting with my accountability group on WhatsApp. A daily prayer journey of praise, confession, invitation for a fresh baptism of the Holy Spirit for character and gifting, prayers for salvation, healing and miracles. Being in an accountability group in daily touch plus a spiritual director. Teaching what I'm discovering to others so it goes deeper in me. Spending time with non-Christians exploring life and faith to stretch my thinking.
>
> (Matt Summerfield, Zeo Church, Hitchin, Reboot Your Leadership)

loves to invite people to his home to eat. He has his disciples there with him. He is with outcasts, sinners, tax collectors – his community is inclusive. Everyone is learning by listening to Jesus and watching how he lives his life. This is his home. His approach to discipleship is intimate and rooted in the rhythms and habits of everyday life.

After choosing his disciples up the mountain he is back home again in chapter 3. (It is worth noting that in Mark's Gospel Jesus' mission is a combination of circles of travel with durations at home.) This time he can't even eat because there are just too many people there! Some of these are keen to listen and follow him. Some have come from Jerusalem because they think he is demon-possessed. His mother and brothers turn up to take him away because they think he has lost his senses. Jesus contrasts his house with Satan's house. Jesus has come to set people free from the prison-house of Satan and establish a family home where unity will keep it strong and where belonging is defined by whoever does the will of God rather than by blood ties or religious influence.

Even in these few stories of Jesus at home we see that he is redefining family. He takes care to honour his mother and we see his siblings join in and even lead the Church in the book of Acts. But his definition of family is not confined to blood ties. It is all about love and shared life – across and within generations, men and women, powerful and powerless. This is *koinonia* which is fellowship – literally having everything in common. Jesus is emphasising togetherness, mutual care, learning and doing life with one another. He has not called it 'Church' at this point but it looks exactly like the early Church in Acts 2. As Mark proceeds with his account of Jesus' life, he continues to show Jesus in houses. He heals the synagogue official's daughter in the privacy of her home in Mark 5:38-43. He is in faraway territory when a Gentile woman comes to the house where Jesus is staying, almost testing his commitment to radically loving his neighbour in Mark 7:24-30. It is in the house that Jesus then spends private time with his disciples teaching them, challenging them, answering their questions, and rigorously shaping this fledging community of believers in Mark 7:17; 9:28; 9:33; 10:10 and 14:6-9. Wherever there is a place – whether it's where Jesus is living or just visiting – Jesus calls it home, and it is from the small and ordinariness of home that he fulfils his mission. This is encouraging for us. We don't need to have a mortgage, a large house, a traditional family. We can imitate Jesus wherever we are, by forming community among anyone who would like to do the will of the Father.

> When he was alone, the Twelve and the others around him asked him about the parables.
>
> (Mark 4:10)

Being together is the place for deep learning. At this end of these important parables of the kingdom in chapter 4, Mark writes that 'when he was alone with his own disciples, he explained everything' (Mark 4:34). We grow in faith when we worship and we grow when we witness, but there is also this inward dimension that Jesus kept returning to with his disciples. Learning in our hearts happens when we are open and vulnerable, when we allow others to see and know us. There were times when fear and pride revealed themselves in the disciples' hearts when they were together with Jesus. For instance, in chapter 9 they are afraid to ask him about what he is saying about death and resurrection, but they are also vociferously arguing about which of them is the best disciple, and being critical of anyone else who is trying to live life in Jesus' name. Despite enjoying eating together, the disciples still seemed to behave in proud and fearful ways.

If the house in Mark represents where koinonia should happen well, Mark also shows it is the place where good community is also most contested. Like the upward disciplines of worship and prayer or the risk that accompanies the outward dimension of witness, the inward dimension of fellowship does not come easily. We are envious of one another, especially of those that Jesus seems to favour the most. We are afraid to reveal our vulnerabilities and insecurities to others. We are judgemental when some people live out their faith differently or have biblical interpretations that are opposed to ours. The 'thinking in [our] hearts' (Mark 2:8), however hidden we believe it is, bleeds out into our words and behaviour. We stand 'outside' like Jesus' family (Mark 3:31), rather than joining in fully, when we are intimidated or resentful. We are 'indignant' and reproving (Mark 14:4-5) when we see what we consider needless extravagance or when our resources are squandered.

In the case of the disciples, there doesn't seem to be much change over their three-year apprenticeship! I would have thought that improvements in behaviour and attitude would be more obvious. In fact, all these struggles are also shown in the early Church. The epistles often have things to say to brothers and sisters in Christ who are shown to be mean, gossipy, proud and fearful. Nevertheless, the experience of being in Jesus' community clearly modelled something that, in the anointing of the Holy Spirit, came alive in the most wonderful, spiritual, social and practical way. On the day of Pentecost, the Holy Spirit is poured out onto the disciples as they are meeting together in a 'house' (Acts 2:2) and they

> My most effective practices are to remain in fellowship with others who love Jesus, to keep my focus on serving others, and to humbly serve both the local church and those who are lost.
>
> (John O'Connor, Junction 42)

begin their way of life together as a new church community '*house to house*' (Acts 2:46; 5:42, my emphasis). There is Judas' house, Cornelius' house, Simon's house, Lydia's house, Crispus' house, the jailer's house, Mary's house and Titius Justus' house – all places where the gospel was learned, expressed and lived out by disciples who were loving and caring for each other. And then of course are all the households which were church communities mentioned in Paul's letters. The biblical account of disciples attempting to be in community is full of examples of both failure and success. The failures show us how real the disciples were, just like us. We can learn from their mistakes and from the way that Jesus and the Holy Spirit taught them. The successes demonstrate that being in Jesus-centred community is possible. It is not a forlorn dream but is the plan of God – from Moses to Jesus. It is the way that God has designed us to be, so that when we submit to his teaching and his ethos, being a member of the family of God, in the house of God, really works. It is enjoyable, meaningful and attractive to everyone around.

> My most effective practice is to start the day with the 321 Daily retreat. This is a simple way to engage with God. Three Minutes read the Bible, take a small passage and read it over a few times. Then ask yourself what changes today because you read this passage.
>
> Two Minutes pray and tell God what is going on in your life. One minute listen to God, is he wanting to say anything to you for the day ahead, if nothing else let the Holy Spirit rest on you.
>
> (Cris Rogers, Spring Harvest, All Hallows Church Bow, Making Disciples)

Ultimately the house of God is a new temple. Not a building where only one special high priest can enter because of its holiness, but a group of people who are made holy by the Spirit of God, through the kind of process of formation and discipleship that Jesus took his disciples. Notice the language in Paul's letter to the Ephesians. All are welcome, as we saw in Deuteronomy and the ministry of Jesus, and there are various words for house: household, dwelling, building and temple, all which emphasise that the household of God is where the new family are the ones who do the will of the Father.

> Consequently, you are no longer foreigners and strangers, but fellow citizens with God's people and also members of his household, built on the foundation of the apostles and prophets, with Christ Jesus himself as the chief cornerstone. In him the whole building is joined together and rises to become a holy temple in the Lord. And in him you too are being built together to become a dwelling in which God lives by his Spirit.
>
> (Ephesians 2:19-22)

No wonder, then that the Hebrew word for 'heart' has the idea of house within it. No wonder that Jacob calls the place where he meets with God 'Bethel', 'the house of God' (Genesis 28:17). And no wonder that the psalmist wishes to live in the 'house of the Lord' forever (Psalm 27:4). This is where we all belong, in community, brothers and sisters of Jesus Christ himself who has given us new hearts, together doing the will of the Father.

> My most effective practices include memorising Scripture, early morning prayer walking, rigorous accountability partners, journaling, reading Bible through the Year, sharing faith.
>
> (Simon Guillebaud, Speaker and Author, Great Lakes Outreach, Burundi)

John 15:12-17 raises a tension within us that needs some unpacking. Jesus calls us 'friends' and yet he is both Lord and Saviour, what does this mean for us in our real lives? In ancient times there was a sense in which a king would surround himself with some advisors who became 'friends of the king'. He was still the king and they were still the subjects but there was relationship, there was a sharing of thoughts, hopes and ideas.

If we are truly 'friends of the King' we have an allegiance to that king which means we want to do what pleases him, not because we have to but because we want to. Ultimately that is expressed in how we love one another, love is the hallmark of what is means to be a follower of Jesus. It's the ultimate apologetic to a watching and, at times, sceptical world. It means we express that love in lives of service as Jesus did. Love is not an emotion, it's an action. It's not an adjective it's a verb; it's what we do that evidences who we know. The key part of the phrase Jesus gives us in this command is 'as I have loved you' (John 13:34). This sets the bar for the kind of love we are to model out between us and to others outside of our community. It's not a mirror of our human and at times fickle love but it's sacrificial love, the kind Jesus lived out for us on the cross. To know the Master's business means we are aware of the kingdom of God and what that means lived out in our daily lives as individuals and corporately together. The fruit that remains will not be our buildings, our programmes and our projects but the way we love people through those things and at times in spite of those things.

(Leon Evans, Lifecentral Church, Further Faster Network)

Living Room

Heart ethos

Discipleship is daily choosing to be like Jesus. Not so much just trying to follow the rules but having faith in the love of God, loving him in such a way that we want to fulfil the law. In Ezekiel and Jeremiah these laws are not on stone tablets, or in a rule book, but they are written on hearts. Therefore, living well in community, learning and following Jesus together as disciples, is essentially a heart issue. We often say to one another, 'Eat to your heart's content.' Wine gladdens the heart, oil makes the face shine, and bread 'sustains . . . hearts' (Psalm 104:15). Wine theologian, Dr Gisela Kreglinger, points to 1 Kings 4:25 as the fulfilment of the love expressed in the great commandments of Deuteronomy 6 and Leviticus 19:[75] 'During Solomon's lifetime Judah and Israel, from Dan to Beersheba, lived in safety, everyone under their own vine and under their own fig-tree.'

It is in their farming that they learned to be God's people, and she highlights archeological evidence that these small family farms would have produced about 694 litres of wine a year. That's quite a lot of wine! Even if Zechariah 3:10 is followed when we invite our neighbour over to share some of those bottles, there are some very glad hearts there.

Social ethos

Deuteronomy is an interesting combination of national rules and laws for the sake of a just and well-ordered society, along with its emphasis on gathering, eating, being a mixed 'family' group, and including all ages. Mark's Gospel, as we have seen, has its emphasis on community that can fit in a house – or at least squeeze in, block the kitchen and create temporary

75. Gisela Kreglinger, *Cup Overflowing* (Nashville, TN: HarperChristian Resources), p. 30.

rooftop terraces. And even outside of the house, Jesus treats those who follow him like a family who need gathering, caring for and feeding.

It is no surprise then that the early Church made sure they were eating together regularly, with 'glad and sincere hearts' (Acts 2:46). Glad here means exuberant! That's a feast or a party. Sincere means simple. So it is a combination of simplicity and great joy. Not much money needs to be spent to have a meaningful and intimate time with those who you are close to. Notice, too, that hearts are referred to. The eating together is more about the heart than the food itself. Ecclesiastes, which shows something of how humans are designed to live as they search for meaning, says: 'Go then, eat your bread in happiness and drink your wine with a cheerful heart' (Ecclesiastes 9:7, NASB1995).

> Being an everything-all-the-time kind of person means that I have a tendency to burn out. One of the things that Jesus says that I particularly love, is when he told people that unlike other rabbis, his teachings (yoke) was 'easy and . . . light' (Matthew 11:30). How many of us Christians have grasped the enormous liberty in that statement! As I've matured in my faith (and years!), I have revelled in the realisation that when Jesus stepped away from the crowd for solitude and when he enjoyed good food, wine and company with friends – he was modelling the deep relationships with Father God and with our fellow humans that nourish, sustain and inspire new acts of Kingdom bringing mission.
>
> (Clare Walker, Stewardship)

Hospitality

An important part of our relating together as brothers and sisters in Christ, should be done when we're eating together. Preparing the food is creative and communal and full of anticipation. It is a great bonding experience – which is why Martha gets all ratty with her sister for not helping in Luke 10:40. The disciples all pitch in at the feedings of the thousands, and in doing so take part in the miracle of multiplication. Abraham and Gideon prepare meals for angels which results in extraordinary eye-opening God-encounters. Jesus gets everything sorted for the last supper and preps the barbecue for the resurrection beach breakfast. We have already seen that Brother Lawrence found his vocation in the tasks of meal preparation. When Jesus feeds the 5,000 he has recognised their need for a shepherd, for welcome, teaching and healing, and so feeding these people is a practical and spiritual demonstration of this. Moses did a similar thing when manna was given by God in the wilderness. The collection and preparation of these meals was a lesson in trusting God.[76] In Acts 6, the most spirit-filled people were

> I am so thankful that God has put some brilliant friends, mentors in my life to encourage me in my walk with him. Some have been seasonal & some have been constant, I love the fact that as we are being mentored we also have the challenge to mentor others as well. I have always benefited from spending time with people, churches or organisations that are further on than we are, it lifts faith and when I see it, I catch it.
>
> (Dan Hargreaves, Alive Church Lincoln)

76. Exodus 16:4-7.

chosen by the apostles to organise buying, preparing and serving meals to those who didn't have the resource to do it for themselves. It was a strategically spiritual part of the early Church's life.

Part of my father-in-law's journey of faith was joining in a mission team to France and being in charge of buying food for the team. What's not to love about a French supermarket? The *jambon* and the *fromage*! Being a grandfather figure, he was fully part of an all-age team of families, as we served a local church by touring with an evangelistic show. He said that this experience helped him join in with church community.

Serving coffee is as much part of church life as singing worship songs. It is a great way of contributing to church life and ministry – welcoming new people and refreshing disciples. It is also great if you're not sure what to do or who to speak to after a church service – there's a role, probably a name badge, the satisfaction of serving and being kind, and also conversations that can come easily. Being church family together like this, before or after worshipping and praying with each other, is a wonderful way of building friendships and speaking truth in love to one another – which can easily lead to yet more prayer.

Rather than this being a necessary but secondary part of community living, it is worth putting effort and creativity into the administration and preparation of eating together and discovering the building of relationships as we work alongside one another. Preparing food is such a good way of building team spirit, being part of the Holy Spirit's powerful flow of life, and preparing us for ministry in other spheres.

Eating together

It is round the table that we can be open and honest, that deep conversation can happen and good and meaningful questions can be asked. The Last Supper is a good example of this – where Jesus is honest and where the disciples' hearts are revealed. Jesus also saw that the way to show true welcome was to eat with people – especially to demonstrate kindness to those who were shunned for whatever reason. He is seen and criticised for eating with 'sinners' – those who are irreligious, or living obviously in an immoral way, and 'tax collectors' – those who are betraying their own people (Matthew 9:10-11; 11:19). But it is this very act of hospitality that demonstrates so fully the gospel of the kingdom of heaven. Zacchaeus was forgiven, released and set free countless others in Jericho because of a shared meal with Jesus. The woman who anointed Jesus at Bethany was honoured for her worship beyond any other guests at that meal. Sharing a drink of water at the well transformed the woman who chatted with Jesus, and also her whole village. Peter's rumbling tummy opened his imagination to hear from God which led to him inviting gentiles to stay as guests overnight, and then him going with them for a return sleepover at their house – followed by an outpouring of the Holy Spirit.[77]

> My best experience has been when I have met with like-minded people on a regular basis, digging into Scripture together, sharing our hearts, being vulnerable, being brutally honest and holding each other accountable. It's transformational!
>
> (Damian Wharton, Scripture Union Northern Ireland)

77. Luke 19:1-10; Mark 14:3-9; John 4:7-43; Acts 10:1-48.

I wonder why eating together is so intimate, warm and barrier breaking? Although the kingdom of heaven is not only 'a matter of eating and drinking, but righteousness, peace and joy in the Holy Spirit' (Romans 14:17), it is so very similar and intricately linked because of the qualities of sharing a meal together. Sharing is an example of true *shalom*. Thankfulness bubbles up because our bodies are so grateful and our tastebuds so satisfied. Satisfaction itself – being fed after being hungry – is a significant metaphor all through Scripture for the compassion of God towards us. And taste is a similar physical attribute that speaks to us about the way our hearts receive goodness. We are able to look at each other but also break off at times to concentrate on our plates. There is just the right amount of gaze and just the right amount of reflection to make us feel both stimulated and at ease. Conversation happens in a way that may be less threatening than other contexts but is still very honest. Eating together is so good for us – it's not surprising that Deuteronomy is full of commands to set aside days and weeks to make sure it's done well. And also not surprising that Jesus uses a shared meal to represent the most significant event in the universe, and to remind us of the beauty and strength of his sacrificial love for us.

Effective disciplines for me have been reaching out and supporting others and seeing them grow in their faith. Daily putting on the armour of God, especially Ephesians 6:16 (TPT): 'In every battle, take faith as your wrap-around shield, for it is able to extinguish the blazing arrows coming at you from the evil one!' Being ready to stand firm in difficult situations and then see the Lord work, his way not ours!

(Rosie Giles, Spring Harvest)

So, how much eating are we doing with one another as disciples? How does your Christian community make room for hospitality? The Alpha course[78] has this built in – the eating as an integral part of learning and journeying together with Jesus. Churches celebrate communion regularly but maybe don't feast enough together, or promote eating together from house to house. Our busy lives often mean that we forego the social ethos for what we think is the spiritual ethos – not realising that they are joined together. We turn up at a church meeting, do the stuff and return home again. Whereas Jesus did his meeting at home around a meal, or if he did go to the synagogue, got back quite quick for lunch with his disciples.

What would it look like to do more breakfasts together? To eat before or after a Sunday gathering? To have Bible study and prayer during and round a meal? To have more of an open house like Jesus did? It is worth thinking through some small changes that deliberately integrate the social ethos of eating and drinking together with our discipleship lives.

Looking after one another as a family: All ages

Loving one another is the way that people will see we are Jesus' disciples.[79] We have seen how Jesus demonstrated this by intentionally spending time with all kinds of people. The rich, the poor, the prominent and the outcast. Most of the stories we have are where Jesus gathers adults and forms community with them. Some are older, like Simon Peter's mother-in-law who is ill, then healed and then serves in the house. Jesus also welcomed children; there was a child present

78. https://alpha.org.uk/ (accessed 3.11.25).
79. John 13:35

when he was at home in Capernaum, when they bring lots of children – probably round to his house – to be blessed, and there is the one generous boy at the feeding of the 5,000.[80] In a similar way, Moses teaching in Deuteronomy is not just focused on adults but intentionally includes children. He says to impress these commands on your children (and grandchildren)[81] and all this is for the good of their children and grandchildren.[82] Everyone is to be gathered:

> men, women and children, and the foreigners residing in your towns—so they can listen and learn to fear the Lord your God and follow carefully all the words of this law. Their children, who do not know this law, must hear it and learn to fear the Lord your God as long as you live in the land you are crossing the Jordan to possess.
>
> (Deuteronomy 31:12-13)

> My life group is very important – having other Christians in my life who can encourage and challenge me, and whom I can encourage and challenge. Being part of a community helps to keep everyone accountable.
>
> I love using art to Bible journal – it helps me to connect to what the Bible teaches and is an important way for me to respond in worship to what God is teaching me. It also provides a beautiful record of my faith journey, and it's incredible to look back and see how God has taught me and answered prayers through my art pieces.
>
> (Janneke Klos, Count Everyone In)

80. Mark 1:30-31.
81. Deuteronomy 4:9; 6:7; 11:17; 32:46.
82. Deuteronomy 4:10,40; 5:29, 6:2; 11:21; 12:25,28; 30:19.

In our society we often separate out the education of children so that we can give them expertise, well-planned teaching, directed and differentiated for needs, abilities and age. Education has become excellent in so many ways. This has also been done in church – as Sunday schools that provided basic education instead of schools, along with a discipleship curriculum, and also in order to help children and teenagers learn and work out their faith with their peers. Spring Harvest is one of many organisations that have excellent children's work and youth work and where in recent years many hundreds of under eighteen's have come to faith and then been trained in faith.

Alongside these positive experiences, it has been harder to integrate church discipleship between the generations. This then leads to expressions of worship and learning that are markedly different between adults and children. It also

> Much of my growth has come through the discipline of renewing my mind. It often begins with our mindset – the thoughts and beliefs we hold about ourselves, others, and what God can do. Ephesians urges us to 'put off the old self' and 'put on the new self' (Ephesians 4:22-24). That practice of intentionally exchanging worn-out thinking for God's truth has been life-changing. The support of a faith-filled community, strong teaching, and tools that help identify false beliefs and replace them with truth have been especially helpful. In the early days of my ministry Rick Warren's *Purpose Driven Life*[83] was formational.
>
> (Gaynor van der Burton, FitFish)

83. Published: Nashville, TN: HarperChristian Resources, 2013.

means there is less time or room to have everyone together in worship and teaching – and when we do, we are not sure about how to go about it well. But what if we could express our worship, our learning, and our looking after one another intergenerationally? Nick and Becky Drake have written a great book on this, *Worship for Everyone: Unlocking the Transforming Power of All-Age Worship*[84] – with theology, theory, practice and resources – in order to help churches worship together across all ages' groups. They point out the times in the Bible where everyone is together – including some of the instances we have seen above; and the moments when there are adults who are fed up with having children praising and worshipping in the time and place where the adults are used to doing this in their own way. The Drakes highlight the irony, described in Matthew 21:12-17, that the temple, which is the place where healing and worship are meant to happen, is now a marketplace. Jesus overturns the tables, the blind and lame come and are healed, and the children start praising and singing 'Hosanna to the Son of David'. Jesus makes room for both adults and children in the temple, and quotes Psalm 8 that God himself calls out praise from the lips of children.[85] Nick and Becky state in Chapter 6 that what is needed for children to join in is 'belonging', 'familiarity', 'acceptance', 'purpose' and 'fun' (which is what Jesus gave them in abundance in that dramatic temple clearing story!)

What does it look like for us to teach our children about Jesus – like Moses said, when we 'sit . . . walk . . . lie down and . . . get up'?[86] How about some home rhythms where this becomes the culture? Are there opportunities for children to serve and find purpose when we gather as church, is a question that Nick and Becky Drake ask. How may we introduce children to the

84. Nick Drake, Becky Drake, *Worship for Everyone: Unlocking the Transforming Power of All-Age Worship* (London: SPCK Publishing, 2021).
85. Ibid, page 40.
86. Deuteronomy 6:7.

way we encounter Jesus in worship and prayer – so they can see how astounded we are, how moved, how deeply we know God's presence and love, and what our passionate praise looks like? It may be that we need to rethink our worship gatherings – perhaps check out Spring Harvest's *The Big Start* where this is done so well, or follow ministries like Worship for Everyone to learn from them.[87]

Looking after one another as a family: Meeting needs

Meeting one another's needs, whether that is physical, social, emotional or spiritual is at the heart of the design of church in the book of Acts. The Church is the example of what life can be like when people invite Jesus and his Spirit to be at the heart of their relationships and purpose. This inward dimension of church life is as important as the upward dimension. The buildings and spaces of the early Church reflected the nature of the Church's identity and mission. Meeting in houses shows how relationships and daily life was important, just as the temple or lecture halls show how worship and evangelism were important. Similarly, the design of Paul's letters also reveals how this inward dimension had high value in his thinking. Much of Paul's writing is about caring for one another. He was introduced to a church that 'had everything in common' where believers sold possessions so the others would not be in need (Acts 2:44,45).

> I have come to believe that the real test is what we do in secret.
>
> (Rob Parsons, Care for the Family)

87. www.worshipforeveryone.com; https://bigstartassemblies.org (accessed 17.11.25)

He later raised money from churches so that those impacted by famine would survive, as we see in Acts 11:27-30.

The inward dimension of loving one another is fully practical. It means caring for one another's needs. Today this may mean helping out one another financially, or giving lifts to appointments or helping with parenting. It will include making meals especially when people are going through crisis or an impactful life event. It will involve sharing possessions – washing machines, lawnmowers, cars and rooms in houses. Church fellowship cannot just be about being friendly and cooperating while we run a church task – although this is a great place to practise love and kindness. It is also about real life. Which is what makes church life, when it's going well, the best thing ever! 'Love one another' is not arduous once the Holy Spirit fills our hearts, minds and souls with his strength. It becomes a self-fulfilling cycle of goodness where one act of kindness inspires another. Sometimes this may feel like it is

> Reflecting on what has helped me live more like Jesus, is like sifting through a highlights reel, where so many things have fed into my discipleship journey. As I reflect, I think about the youth leaders who spent time investing in me as a teenager; the impact that Shane Claiborne's *Irresistible Revolution*[88] had when I first read it; the years I came to Spring Harvest myself with my family; my father's interest in Celtic Christianity turning into my own; the times when journalling has helped me connect profoundly with Jesus; and simply watching the way my mother served others self-sacrificially.
>
> (Bethan Newman, Youth for Christ)

88. Shane Claiborne, *The Irresistible Revolution* (Grand Rapids, MI: Zondervan, 2006).

owed, or done only out of duty. But when our hearts are cleansed of that kind of transactional thinking, mutual affection is wonderful. Fervently 'love one another', writes Peter in 1 Peter 1:22. Paul uses the same word in 1 Thessalonians 4 where he writes: 'Now about your love for one another we do not need to write to you, for you yourselves have been taught by God to love each other.'

This takes us back to the word of God written on our foreheads, our hands, our houses, and certainly now our hearts. It becomes more natural to be selfless than to be selfish.[89] Paul also uses the same word in Romans 12:10-13. Here Paul sums up what the inward dimension of love looks like:

> Be devoted to one another in love. Honour one another above yourselves. Never be lacking in zeal, but keep your spiritual fervour, serving the Lord. Be joyful in hope, patient in affliction, faithful in prayer. Share with the Lord's people who are in need. Practise hospitality.

The habit of fellowship

It is easier to think of spiritual disciplines that are personal, private and upward focused. In his book *Holy Habits*, Andrew Roberts writes about the habit of fellowship,[90] along with serving, giving and glad generosity. These are all interpersonal practices that can only be done in community or for others, and yet are as integral to being a disciple as prayer, solitude and reading the Bible. We are reminded that, like any of the habits, the habit of fellowship does not necessarily come easily. It has to be practiced. Andrew says that seeing this through a romantic lens of tranquility and harmony is misguided. It takes time, is messy, fraught with compromise

89. Deuteronomy 6:8-9; Jeremiah 31:33.
90. Andrew Roberts, *Holy Habits* (Welwyn Garden City: Malcolm Down Publishing, 2020), pp. 129-139.

and struggle. He quotes Pete Greig and Andy Freeman in their book *Punk Monk*, who in turn quote Dietrich Bonhoeffer (all this quoting of each other is a good example of fellowship!), that if community is our aim we may well end up with a superior attitude once we feel we 'have it'.[91] And if the pursuit of community is our main activity, then we will reject outsiders because they upset our balance: our newly found love and acceptance of each other. How many small groups in a church feel they cannot accept a new person because it would ruin what has been achieved? How many churches are so inward-focused and 'friendly' that it is hard to break in to become a fellow member? So, like the other spiritual disciplines,

> Blessed be the tie that binds
> our hearts in Christian love;
> The fellowship of kindred minds
> Is like to that above.
>
> The writer of this hymn was John Fawcett, who was a Baptist minister in Hebden Bridge, a tiny village on a hill. He received a call to a large London church and just as he and his wife were leaving on their loaded cart, she cried out that she couldn't stand leaving! He joined in her cries, unloaded the wagon, and they remained for fifty years. The hymn celebrated their experience of fellowship.
>
> We share each other's woes,
> our mutual burdens bear,
> and often for each other flows
> the sympathizing tear.[92]
>
> (Lisa Holmes, Baptist Union of Scotland)

91. Andy Freeman and Pete Greig, *Punk Monk* (Eastbourne: Kingsway, 2007), p. 100.
92. John Fawcett (1739-1817), 'Blest be the Tie that Binds', https://hymnary.org/text/blest_be_the_tie_that_binds (accessed 17.11.25).

the habit of fellowship can become an idol or a stumbling block even though it is a good thing. Fortunately, the gift of the Holy Spirit means that we are all producing the fruit of the Spirit, and so with some conviction, humility and self-awareness, this means that it is possible to enjoy great community, worked at with diligence, that also welcomes others into its mutual love and serving.

In the house: A story

My wife, Bev, and I always had other people living with us when we were first married. In fact, when our first child was being born in our bedroom on the top floor of the house, from the kitchen I could smell the garlic that a couple of students were cooking with their pasta, oblivious to the contractions of new life happening upstairs. Just over a decade ago, when Bev's dad suddenly died, her mum came to live with us. This extended our household wonderfully, so that we had three generations living and sharing together. All the ironing got done – magically, it seemed! And classic 1970's style meals such as cottage pie and toad-in-the-hole took the place of the previously more exotic Thai curries and prawn and chilli pasta. Bev's mum didn't have to pay bills any more or worry about contracts and maintenance. Living like this is a joy: looking after one another, understanding the differences of lifestyle and expectations, and inviting others of all ages to visit and enjoy this new kind of household. Then a few years ago Social Services approached our church asking for help with Unaccompanied Asylum Seeking Children, as there were lots of them in our town. Frustratingly at that point we didn't have any room, but a couple of years later, as Supported Lodging hosts, we were able to take in a teenager who had been in care. This has added yet another dimension to our household. Unfortunately, Grandma no longer is able to do the ironing or cooking (no more puddings and custard, but plenty more creased clothes). But we have had the privilege of helping prepare one teenager to get their own place and now have another who lives with us. Generally this has meant many more chicken nuggets, coke, sushi and McDonald's. We are now challenged with organising carers and hospital appointments, universal credit and morning alarm clocks. But it has also brought with it energy, compassion, friendship and learning. Our household is our primary place of evangelism and compassion. It is challenging but also what we know we are called to right now. It is where we can practise the inward dimension of discipleship: being 'joyful in hope, patient in affliction, [and] faithful in prayer' (Romans 12:13-14).

There is no greater life than one that is honestly and willingly open to Jesus and to those around us. What does wholehearted discipleship 'in the house' mean to you?

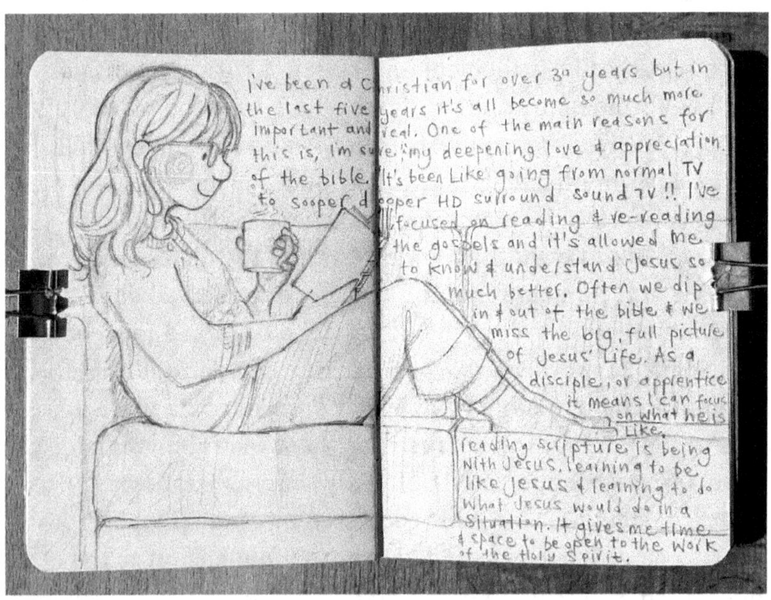

Artist: Ruth Hearson

Playground

For all the resources, links and information about the contributors mentioned, scan the code to visit:

www.springharvest.org/resources/no-greater-life/

Practices

Explore some practices that help us to be more like him as we love one another: Fasting, feasting, celebration, hospitality, prayer, time, generosity, prophecy.

Resources

See also books and courses that help identify gifting and how to serve the body of Christ, such as:

Ruth Hayley Barton, *Sacred Rhythms: Arranging Our Lives for Spiritual Transformation* (Downers Grove, IL: IVP, 2006)

Richard Foster, *Celebration of Discipline* (London: Hodder & Stoughton, 2008)

John Ortberg, Ruth Hayley Barton, *An Ordinary Day with Jesus* (Grand Rapids, MI: Zondervan, 2001)

Jo Swinney and Miranda Harris, *A Place at the Table* (London: Hodder & Stoughton, 2023)

Donald S. Whitney, *Spiritual Disciplines for the Christian Life* (Carol Stream, IL: Tyndale House Publishers, 2014)

Dallas Willard, *The Spirit of the Disciplines* (San Francisco, CA: HarperSanFrancisco, 2025)

https://5qcentral.com/

Guided prayer

To deal with the heart issues and spiritual freedom through praying with others, explore these resources:

www.mercyuk.org/keystofreedom

www.emotionallyhealthy.org/

Lectio Divina 3

Called
Mark 3:13-19

Let's pause and pray with a *Lectio 365* Morning Prayer, meditating on the community of people Jesus chose to spend time with.

Together we will pray (P.R.A.Y.): P – pausing to be still, R – rejoicing with a psalm and reflecting on Scripture, A – asking God to help us and others and Y – yielding to his will in our lives.

Pause

As I enter prayer now, I pause to be still; to breathe slowly, to re-centre my scattered senses upon the presence of God.

Pause and pray

Prayer of Approach

Jesus, I fix my eyes on you, the author and perfecter of my story.
Help me know you more clearly, love you more dearly,
and follow you more nearly, each and every day.[93]

93. Adapted from Hebrews 12:2 and the prayer of Richard of Chichester, www.lords-prayer-words.com/famous_prayers/day_by_day_lyrics_prayer_st_richard.html (accessed 28.11.25).

Rejoice and reflect

I choose to rejoice in God's unshakable love today, joining with the ancient praise of all God's people in the words of Psalm 33:

> . . . the LORD's plans stand firm forever;
> his intentions can never be shaken.
>
> What joy for the nation whose God is the LORD,
> whose people he has chosen as his inheritance.
>
> (Psalm 33:11-12, NLT)

Pause and pray

I reflect on the community of friends and disciples with whom Jesus chose to share his life, his love and his life-changing mission:

> Jesus went up on a mountainside and called to him those he wanted, and they came to him. He appointed twelve that they might be with him and that he might send them out to preach and to have authority to drive out demons. These are the twelve he appointed: Simon (to whom he gave the name Peter), James son of Zebedee and his brother John (to them he gave the name Boanerges, which means 'sons of thunder'), Andrew, Philip, Bartholomew, Matthew, Thomas, James son of Alphaeus, Thaddaeus, Simon the Zealot and Judas Iscariot, who betrayed him.
>
> (Mark 3:13-19)

Jesus was choosing the people with whom he would share his most powerful *and* his most vulnerable moments. Each disciple would receive ground-breaking teaching, join a world-changing mission and gain intimate access to Jesus himself. For this honour Jesus selects some surprising people. He starts with Peter, the friend who would one day deny him. He continues with a list that includes Matthew (a traitor) and

Simon (a zealot). Then Jesus finishes with Judas, the disciple who would hand him over to be executed! They're not exactly a dream team, but Mark says 'he wanted' them all.

Ask

Jesus extends the same invitation to me. He *wants me* to 'be with him . . . that he might send [me] out'. Is there anything I think disqualifies me?

Jesus, Rabbi to flawed followers, I bring you my insecurity and I choose to accept your invitation.

Pause and pray

Jesus makes disciples who in turn make disciples; sharing what they've experienced and learned about the love of God with others. Who am I discipling?

Jesus, how can I build them up and encourage them today?

Pause and pray

Yield

As I return to today's passage, I pay particular attention to my feelings as I read these words.

> Jesus went up on a mountainside and called to him those he wanted, and they came to him. He appointed twelve that they might be with him and that he might send them out to preach and to have authority to drive out demons. These are the twelve he appointed: Simon (to whom he gave the name Peter), James son of Zebedee and his brother John (to them he gave the name Boanerges, which means 'sons of thunder'), Andrew, Philip, Bartholomew,

> Matthew, Thomas, James son of Alphaeus, Thaddaeus, Simon the Zealot and Judas Iscariot, who betrayed him.
>
> (Mark 3:13-19)

I take a moment now to reflect on any particular feeling stirred within me by this passage.

Pause

I wonder how well the disciples got on with each other. There seems to have been some strong personalities and probably very different perspectives in that group. It reminds me of the beauty and challenge of my church community. Where else do I gather with people of different ages, ethnicities and economic backgrounds, with different professions, family shapes and political perspectives? Together we are united by our love for Christ, and we are growing in our love for and understanding of each other.

Pause and pray

Yielding Prayer

Jesus, I confess that I don't always find the people I worship next to easy. But I'm not always easy to love either! Thank you that you've chosen us all. As we move closer to you, would you draw us closer to each other?

Yielding Promise

And now, as I prepare to take this time of prayer into the coming day, the Lord who loves me says in the Gospel of John:

> You did not choose me, but I chose you and appointed you so that you might go and bear fruit – fruit that will last . . .
>
> (John 15:16a)

Closing prayer

Father, help me to live this day to the full,
being true to you in every way.
Jesus, help me to give myself away to others,
being kind to everyone I meet.
Spirit, help me to love the lost,
proclaiming Christ in all I do and say.

Amen

Lectio 365 is a prayer app from 24-7 Prayer. Download for free to pray the Bible morning, noon and night.

Further Bible verses to read and reflect on

John 13:34,35; John 15:8-12; Deuteronomy 4:5-9

Journal – pray, reflect, write

Find some people to journey with!

Who are they and how will you love deeply with them?

....

....

....

Write down their names and begin to pray for them. What comes to mind when you pray – write this down. (Should you share it with them – will it encourage them and help them become closer to Jesus?)

....

....

....

Read the story of the disciples on the road to Emmaus in Luke 24:13-35. How does this story speak into how you might develop new Christ-centred relationships with these people whose names you have written down?

....

....

....

Action

Not all of us have the flexibility or resource to invite people in for fellowship, but see whether any of these activities inspire you.

- How will you use your home or room for Christian community? Or could you use another space and invite someone to join you in a café or pub?
- Schedule some gathered events or plan moments and activities of fellowship and serving. This could be on a walk, in a park, at the library, in a common room – or perhaps in someone's home or in a church space.
- Pop in to a friend's house unannounced. (Is this OK to do now, or do you have to message first, do you think?)
- If you have your own place or room, invite more people than is comfortable, to see what Jesus felt like!

- Who is in need of a meal that you could make and take round? Someone who is under pressure, a mother who has just had a baby, a family who are grieving . . .
- Start reading the Bible together with a few other people.

Group Bible study

A tale of two crowded homes

Read Mark 2:1-13 and Mark 3:20-35

In both stories Jesus is at home and it's crowded, but we will see the difference between Jesus' family, the teachers of the law and then the ordinary people who want to be with and like Jesus.

- How do you think Jesus felt when the religious experts criticised him in his own house (2:6-7 and 3:22)? How do you cope with negativity?
- What did the man and his four friends have that the teachers of the law and Jesus' family not have? Talk about how this is not to do with religious knowledge/ experience nor social proximity to Jesus and what that means for our own position or how we see others.
- Compare the friends' visibility and the lame man's vulnerability of publicly having his sins forgiven with Jesus' family standing outside and sending for him. When have you either been committed or vulnerable in relationships, or embarrassed and distancing?
- In what ways does Satan establish sinful power and negativity in community?
- Where are the disciples in each of these stories?

- Discuss together how this story defines friendship, family and discipleship.
- Pray together for soft hearts, the gift of encouragement and the desire to simply do the will of the Father.

Wholehearted – a series of studies about the heart #3

Ezekiel prophesies the outpouring of the Holy Spirit that gives a new heart and enables us to follow God's commands:

> I will give you a new heart and put a new spirit in you; I will remove from you your heart of stone and give you a heart of flesh. And I will put my Spirit in you and move you to follow my decrees and be careful to keep my laws.
>
> (Ezekiel 36:26-27)

This follows a similar earlier prophecy of Ezekiel's in chapter 11:

> I will give them an undivided heart and put a new spirit in them; I will remove from them their heart of stone and give them a heart of flesh. Then they will follow my decrees and be careful to keep my laws. They will be my people, and I will be their God. But as for those whose hearts are devoted to their vile images and detestable idols, I will bring down on their own heads what they have done, declares the Sovereign Lord.

Jeremiah 31:33-34 has a similar vision for everyone – from the least to the greatest – quoted also in Hebrews 8.

'This is the covenant I will make with the people of Israel after that time,' declares the LORD. 'I will put my law in their minds and write it on their hearts. I will be their God, and they will be my people. No longer will they teach their neighbour, or say to one another, 'Know the LORD,' because they will all know me, from the least of them to the greatest,' declares the LORD. 'For I will forgive their wickedness and will remember their sins no more.'

The Apostle Paul picks up this idea, too, in 2 Corinthians 3:2-3:

> You yourselves are our letter, written on our hearts, known and read by everyone. You show that you are a letter from Christ, the result of our ministry, written not with ink but with the Spirit of the living God, not on tablets of stone but on tablets of human hearts.

This image of the heart of flesh, with God's word written into it, emphasises the vulnerability but aliveness of the human heart. The word 'flesh' in Hebrew is '*basar*', a word for humanity and also for meat! (Its nearest equivalent in Greek is *sarx*.) We are frail and yet our hearts beat with life – more so than a tablet of stone. In Genesis 2:23 when Adams sees Eve, he cries out with delight: 'Flesh of my flesh' – meaning, 'You are like me, I can relate to you.' And they become 'one flesh', a new identity is formed. In John 1, Jesus is 'the Word [become] flesh', John's own interpretation of the law of God now living and breathing in a human heart. We, too, can say 'flesh of my flesh' when we look at Jesus. He is like us! Jesus refers to himself as the Son of Man rather than the Son of God in Mark's Gospel. This shows that God's intention for his justice, righteousness and love has always been to be fleshed out in the human heart. Jesus is now the new Adam, the new human with a soft heart, and his desire is that we too can have hearts of flesh that display his words for the world to see. His aim, like the unity between Adam and Eve in Genesis 2, is for us to be in him, our lives be 'hidden with Christ in God' (Colossians 3:3). We are in him, new creations, with new and soft hearts, that display his love and beauty.

Questions

Read the Bible verses above. In what ways is the Word of God written on your own hearts?

How can you tell that this Word is 'richly' dwelling in you (Colossians 3:16)?

Three times in Hebrews we are reminded not to harden our hearts – see 3:8,15 and 4:7. How do we know when our hearts are hardening – what are the signs of this in our lives?

The writer of Hebrews says to 'encourage one another daily' (3:13) to address this. How can we encourage each other to remain soft-hearted?

A soft heart is easily hurt and damaged. We may harden our hearts to protect ourselves from this or perhaps because we are looking for satisfaction away from the things of God. Think about – or if you are with others, share together – the kinds of things undermine your trust in God and cause you to put up the defences, or that draw you away from God and his people.

What is the most important word of God that is written on your heart at the moment?

Pray (if you are in a group for each other), to firmly hold to your conviction and to softly offer your heart to the love of the Father.

Artist: Debs Last

As an artist, I find myself in a uniquely wonderful position – able to connect as a creative with the Creator God. Faith is sometimes portrayed as a deeply academic pursuit, and while it's vital that we use our intellect to explore and examine it, I feel incredibly blessed to engage with what Makoto Fujimura calls the 'Theology of Making'.[94] This practice and discipline connects me with God in a deeply creative and contemplative way.

94. Makoto Fujimura, *Art and Faith: A Theology of Making* (New Haven, CT: Yale University Press, 2021).

I make art in the tradition of making that echoes God's own: 'Let us make . . .' – a beautiful coming together of thoughts, ideas, and inspiration that moves into the act of creating. I create, hopefully in partnership with God, as we playfully explore an idea, a moment, a thought, and bring it into being as a physical work.

At the beginning of my journey as a full-time artist, I was recommended *The Artist's Way* by Julia Cameron.[95] It introduced me to the daily practice of writing morning pages and reminded me of the importance of daily walks – both of which have become central to my times of contemplation and quiet with Jesus. But perhaps the most transformative idea Cameron introduced was the concept of a weekly 'artist date' – time spent alone with your inner artist (and, for me, with Jesus), centred around joy and play. When life gets busy, these are the first practices to slip away, and life always feels poorer without them.

Sometimes an artist date is as simple as visiting a gallery alone or sitting quietly in an ancient, empty church. Other times it's bringing playful materials into the studio. Some of my best moments have come from sitting on my studio floor, crumbling charcoal onto paper, spreading it with the flat of my hand – not making anything 'serious', but discovering artwork I didn't know was within me. These are the moments when I step aside and allow the Spirit to speak. I often wonder what Jesus wrote or drew in the sand – was it a silent act of expression, a piece of performance art? His whole body moving with the action of making. A challenge, and an inspiration.

My artistic practices are woven into my faith practices. Most mornings, I wake early, make tea, and go to a

95. Published London: Pan Books, 1995.

space I've made beautiful – a candle, a comfy chair. I stream-write my morning pages, read Scripture and pray. It's quiet, grounding, and sets the tone for my day, whether I'm heading to the studio or leading an adult art workshop. There are no rules – if I miss a morning, I don't feel guilty. It's not a duty, it's a joy. A habit.

I've loved reading John Mark Comer, particularly *Practicing the Way*,[96] which helped me embed spiritual disciplines as part of my daily rhythm – not as burdens, but as pleasures. The most freeing thing I've learned from his writing is this: the King of kings, Jesus, waits quietly to spend time with me – looking at me with love, ready to send me into my day inspired and grounded in his affection.

One of the most important things I've learned, both as a creative and as a Christian, is that things rarely go as planned. Sometimes that's painful. Sometimes, a happy accident becomes the making of a painting. If our hope of heaven – a place of greater beauty, adventure, and discovery than earth – is true, then we'll have time to understand, to figure things out. For now, we keep finding our way, doing our best, and learning to play.

(Debs Last)

96. Colorado Springs, CO: WaterBrook Press, 2024.

PART FOUR

Out To The World

**Looking out:
to love Jesus and our
neighbours in our mission**

Classroom

When we love him wholly, from the inside out, we love others as ourselves and our relationship with him has an impact in the world. God doesn't just love us (his Christian people). He loves and cares for everyone, the whole world, and longs to draw them all in, to graft them all into Jesus, along with us his church. He is outward-looking – seeing need and receiving all who come to him.

The Greatest Commandment in Mark 12 shows the shape and content of the power of faith in Jesus. Firstly, there is a call to look up to God and recognise his power, and then give ourselves in love to him. Then comes the way we share that love with one another, including the 'other'; the neighbour who is not necessarily part of our faith family. If all we had was Leviticus 19:18, 'Love your neighbour as yourself', without the filling of love and power, then it would be very hard to 'do to others what [we would like them to do to us]' (Matthew 7:12). In Christ this is not only possible, however, but it is inevitable. Love fills the shape of this command and cascades out from it.

The ultimate love we read about in the Bible is the love of God that sets us free from the power of sin and gives us eternal life: 'But God demonstrates his own love for us in this: while we were still sinners, Christ died for us' (Romans 5:8). Paul goes on to write about the extraordinary salvation and God's abundant provision of grace and righteousness. This is eternal life, starting now, and not only assuring us of an incredible future with Jesus, but also a way of reigning with Christ in life now, experiencing his goodness and giving it away to others. This kind of love compels us to live for Jesus, to imitate him in seeing people set free from sin and death and inherit eternal life. Of course, Jesus had his eye on the future where people from every tribe, tongue and nation will reign with him in eternity, but his kingdom gospel also brought that future into people's everyday here and now. The same power that was to raise Jesus from the dead, through his earthly ministry, healed people, delivered them, sorted out their relationships and their mental health. This good news, preached as a manifesto in the synagogue in Nazareth and recorded in Luke 4, was spiritually, socially, physically and emotionally effective. In the same way, when we are compelled by the love of Jesus we become Christ's ambassadors – living, speaking, acting like him; bringing life wherever we go – a message of hope, power and reconciliation for people's lives now and their eternal future. There's no greater life than this!

> But here's the thing. A lot of the people I work with – they don't know what real love even looks like (like me). They've been battered, bruised, let down by life. Some of them think love's about paying for it, or earning it, or behaving right so you don't get abandoned. And then we come in saying, 'Jesus loves you just as you are,' and it's hard for them to believe. But that's where it starts. Jesus doesn't say, 'You've got to do this, this, and this to be loved.' He says, 'Love God with all your heart.'[97] And when you love someone proper, you don't have to prove it – they just know. I've got a wife, Natasha, two young men, and now a granddaughter, and I don't need to convince them I love them. They see it in how I am. That's what evangelism is to me. Not standing on a soapbox shouting. It's about *living* in a way that shows Jesus off. Loving people, being real, listening, caring – it's that simple. If Jesus lives in you, people should see it in how you carry yourself.
>
> (Gram Seed, Sowing Seeds Ministries)

97. See Matthew 22:37.

In his history of the first few centuries of Church growth, *The Rise of Christianity*, Rodney Stark writes that it is this desire for love, justice and humility that sets Christianity apart from other faiths.[98] In the face of terrible sickness that swept the Roman Empire, Christianity not only had good apologetics and ethical teaching but its love in action actually made a difference. He comments that fourth-century emperor Julian complained that the Christians looked after their own poor and everyone else's too, making his rule look ineffectual! Stark also mentions that Church father, Tertullian, was of the opinion that it was the care of the helpless and brotherly kindness that branded Christians in the eyes of their opponents.[99] Stark claims that it was this kindness, this active love in action, combined with justice for women, a sacrificial ethos, fairness across class divides and organised attention to societal chaos, that meant the church grew exponentially. He concludes that the church demonstrated true humanity. Which surely is the right and natural response to having a Saviour who is the Word made flesh and the true Son of Man: humanity as it was designed to be.

> To be missional is to be Christlike. Mission is not just an activity of God; it's part of his DNA. Part of the great invitation of discipleship is to join in with what the Spirit is doing in the world, and as we do so we not only reflect the person of Jesus to the world, but through mission we become more like Jesus.
>
> (Phil Knox, Speaker and Author, Evangelical Alliance)

98. Rodney Stark, *The Rise of Christianity* (San Francisco, CA: HarperSan Francisco, 1997).
99. Stark, *The Rise of Christianity*, pp. 82-88.

Looking out, as God's Deuteronomy people, to the world

There is always a push outwards in the Bible – from Eden, the mountain, the temple – to the promised land and indeed the whole earth. Moses starts his teaching in Deuteronomy 1:6 by saying 'Yahweh our God', just like he starts the prayer. He is always declaring that the God of the universe and all spiritual powers – 'Elohim' – is also the Lord; 'Yahweh' – close, personal, knowable and yet full of never-ending always-to-be-explored mystery. This is the message of Israel, that the one true God is their God and they are his people; that this God, the creator of the universe, is humanity's God and we are all his children. We have already seen in Deuteronomy 4 that having Israel as God's special people is so that the nations will see what it is like to have God in the midst. His greatness shines with glory and majesty; his wonderful voice speaks 'from the fire' (Deuteronomy 5:24). The mission of the people of God is to demonstrate the reality of God's glory and might – to get out there and shine brilliantly like stars in the universe.[100]

Moses immediately reminds the people what God said from Mount Horeb:

> You have stayed long enough at this mountain. Break camp and advance into the hill country of the Amorites; go to all the neighboring peoples in the Arabah, in the mountains, in the western foothills, in the Negev and along the coast, to the land of the Canaanites and to Lebanon, as far as the great river, the Euphrates. See, I have given you this land . . .'
>
> (Deuteronomy 1:6-8)

100. See Philippians 2:15.

Mountains are a wonderful place to encounter God and worship him. Staying there with one another creates community and family. But the first thing God says in Deuteronomy is, 'You have stayed long enough at this mountain'! There are places to explore and people to meet! There is a similar mission given to humanity in Genesis 2, to cultivate and keep the garden with a wider description of this same geography that is waiting to be enjoyed. We have seen that this is broadened out to include all the families of the earth, and there are glimpses on the way of the mythical exoticism of Africa in Sheba and Cush, and of Europe in Tarshish. (I was born in Birmingham and sadly that city doesn't get a mention in the Bible.)

> Look around from where you are, to the north and south, to the east and west. All the land that you see I will give to you and your offspring for ever.
>
> (Genesis 13:14-15)

> People will come from east and west and north and south, and will take their places at the feast in the kingdom of God.
>
> (Luke 13:29)

Count Everyone In[101] is convinced that no one should miss out on Jesus. The gospel is for everyone, and can be understood by everyone, but adults with learning disabilities may need support to grasp it for themselves. Let's not limit what God can do in and through the lives of our friends with learning disabilities. We support churches to think about how they can make the gospel more accessible – through resources, training and celebrations at Spring Harvest.

(Janneke Klos, Count Everyone In)

101. www.counteveryonein.org.uk/ (accessed 17.11.25)

Moses organises for growth and appoints elders to help govern and lead this new people. Unfortunately, however, this first outward push is stalled. The twelve spies go out on mission but most of them return with fear and trembling despite the wonderful potential they have seen. There is another thirty-eight years of wandering, including some more times of worship to receive from the goodness of God, and more challenges to community life to live out the new ethos that God has given in his Ten Commandments. But in Deuteronomy 2:3 we read a repeated command to Go: 'You have circled this mountain long enough. Now turn north' (NASB1995). It is not God's intention for us to only be with him and with one another; there is a mission to bring the ethos of the kingdom of heaven into the whole earth and to prepare earth for a heavenly existence. This time, for Moses, the people really will be moving up and out, so he readies them all with his teaching in Deuteronomy as they cross over the Zered valley and camp by the side of the Jordan river.

What stops Israel from obeying and possessing the promised land?

The wilderness journey, described in Exodus, Numbers, Leviticus and Deuteronomy is so similar to our own discipleship journey, where the issues of our heart often prevent us from fulfilling the great commandment to love God, one another and the world around us. This is usually to do with fear and pride that are lodged in our hearts. Joshua and Caleb, two of the twelve spies, were excited by the prospect of the mission of God. The other ten were fearful and did not want to risk what they already had. This fear spread to all the people who then grumbled and rebelled, which meant they were not only fearful but proud, too![102] They were too

102. Numbers 13:25 – 14:4.

aware of how they thought they would be seen by the peoples of the land. They assumed it would be too big a task. They let emotion overwhelm them and blamed God for saving them for no good reason, deciding that they knew best and would find a way back with a new leader. This is not so different from the attitude of the disciples before Jesus sends them out to care for, heal and witness to others. At the end of Luke 9, they have just tried to cast out a demon from a boy but with little effect. They are afraid to talk about Jesus' about what will happen to him. They argue about who is the greatest. They are jealous of others' success in ministry. They are offended by rejection from Samaritans. They don't want to leave the security of others at home. Similarly, the Israelites say sorry for not following Caleb and Joshua but then decide to do mission in their own way, presumptuously, and make a complete hash of it.[103]

The outward dimension is as much to do with our hearts as the upward and inward dimensions. It is not just a task that has to get done once we've prayed a bit and done some group Bible study with coffee and homemade cake. The mission of Jesus is to love our neighbour – which is a heart mission, albeit expressed practically and with spiritual aims. Loving them like the Father, in the name of Jesus, and in the power of the Spirit,

> Following Jesus in society looks like having missional-incarnational communities: Intentionally living out Jesus' way in a specific neighbourhood or network, addressing social injustice and embedding oneself within the local context and building relationships with neighbours.
>
> (Alan Charter, Children Everywhere Walking With Jesus)

103. Numbers 14:39-45.

will likely impact them in such a way that they really do want to explore the source of this love and the promise of being adopted into God's family and inheriting eternal life.

Unsurprisingly, it is love that gets hindered by the disciples' and Israelites' fear and pride. Even Moses and Aaron find that their mission to possess the promised land is compromised by character failure. Aaron tends to be fearful of the people. He helps them make a golden calf to worship, and he is complicit with Moses when Moses disobeys God's instruction by hitting the rock and not speaking to it.[104] Being afraid of others hinders our love. Of course we should accommodate, which is a strength of Aaron's in his leadership. But, ironically, loving our neighbour may well make us enemies. Jesus had opponents who did not like his love for the poor, women, the ill and the immoral. Fear of the consequences of mission meant that John Mark turned back from being on Paul's team; and meant that Peter and Barnabas compromised their belief in sharing faith and life with non-Jews.[105] Moses, on the other hand, is prideful and keeps losing his temper! He sees the chaos and sin around him and finds it overwhelming. Although he had been forgiven, even for murder, he finds it hard to deal with the sins of others.

> Discipleship for me is moving beyond belief or a tick box exercise where we tick off various Christian Disciplines to living with deep connection to God and involvement in society. Discipleship involves letting go of ego and living a life of love and awareness of what God is doing and joining in.
>
> (Patrick Regan, OBE, Speaker and Author, Brighter Days)

104. Exodus 32:21-25; Numbers 20:7-12.
105. Acts 15:38; Galatians 2:11-14.

Sometimes he is interceding remarkably on their behalf, and at other times he loses control of his anger towards them. Moses smashes the tablets of stone when he sees the worship of the golden calf. He then grinds up the gold into powder and makes people drink it! That is vengeance for you! Instead of speaking to the rock so that God can show his miraculous power through him, Moses is so frustrated with the people that he hits it like he has done before, demonstrating his own power and might, and implicating Aaron in the process.[106] It is like Peter chopping off the servant's ear in Gethsemane, or the disciples wanting to call down fire on the Samaritans because they don't want Jesus' evangelistic event in their villages.[107] Our righteous anger with the hardness of hearts we see around us, the rejection of Jesus and his Church, or the injustice and oppression that is so terribly prevalent, can motivate us well to intercede, but it can also lead to prideful and aggressive behaviour that is not Christlike and does not inherit the kingdom promises.

What does loving neighbours look like for new-community Israel?

At first glance, we read stories of battle in Deuteronomy such as the defeat of Sihon and Og in chapters 2 and 3 and it looks like Israel's mission is a violent and warlike one rather than a mission of loving their neighbours as themselves. This is a huge theological topic in itself! It is always important to see the whole of God's strategy, perfectly fulfilled in Jesus, when trying to work out the whys and wherefores of difficult bible stories. There is of course spiritual battle all through human history where the loving Creator God is opposed by Satan and every prideful rebellious creature and person. The Bible describes this battle from Genesis to Revelation. These

106. Exodus 32:19-20; Numbers 20:7-12.
107. Mark 14:47; Luke 9:52-54.

Israel stories reveal this battle between a new culture of holiness and the surrounding cultures of violence, idolatry and selfishness. They are also to be read as varieties of literature which use imagery and vocabulary, sometimes even conflicting between different accounts, to stimulate our imagination and understanding, so that we wrestle with the Bible and our experience of life and come closer to trusting in God in the process. In his commentary on Deuteronomy, Chris Wright gives a helpful guide to how Israel must live differently and stand against sin.[108] It is also well worth reading work by Dr Helen Paynter, who has established the Centre for the Study of Bible and Violence,[109] which helps us find a way through the bewilderment of the biblical narratives by trusting and understanding the way that our loving God works in the fallen world.[110] Of course we see it all fulfilled in Jesus whose battle

> ROC has hundreds of examples of expressing the love-your-neighbour mission of Jesus. Here are just a few: A mentor helping a single mum build confidence, one small goal at a time. A Street Angel guiding a vulnerable young person to safety at 2 a.m. – with a cup of water and a kind word. ROC Conversations opening space for people of all backgrounds to share ideas and work together. A festival volunteer gently sharing their faith while picking up litter with a smile.
>
> This is discipleship that doesn't need a pulpit. It just needs your yes.
>
> (Debra Green, Redeeming Our Communities)

108. Wright, *New International Bible Commentary: Deuteronomy.*
109. /www.csbvbristol.org.uk/ (accessed 3.11.25).
110. See books by Dr Paynter such as *God of Violence Yesterday, God of Love Today?* (Abingdon: BRF, 2019) and *The Bible on Violence: A Thick Description* (Sheffield: Sheffield Phoenix Press Ltd., 2020).

was clearly spiritual in nature, and who overcame sin and evil, not with his own violence, but with sacrificial love and faith in the goodness of his heavenly Father.

What we do see emerging in this new community is the beginnings of unlikely neighbours becoming part of the family. This is especially seen in the account of Jericho, where Rahab shows hospitality to the spies, and is not only saved but marries into Israel; and not only that, but she becomes an ancestor of David and Jesus![111] The big view of God is that there would be many Rahab-type redemptions so that ultimately 'every tribe and language and people and nation' are not engaged in bloody battle but are purchased for God by Jesus' blood (Rev 5:9-10). Even the worst enemies to Israel such as Egypt (ironically named Rahab!), Babylon, Tyre and Cush will be named as those who are 'born in Zion' (Psalm 87).

> At Safe Families and Home for Good,[112] we express the gospel through radical hospitality – *philoxenia*, the love of strangers. We welcome children and families into community, offering belonging where there was isolation. Our words affirm the God-given value of every person, especially those whose voices are often unheard. Through works of practical care – a meal, fostering or befriending – we live out Christ's love in action. And in doing so, we witness wonders: families strengthened, children finding stable homes, and hope restored. This is the heart of the gospel, Jesus stepping into our lives and calling us to do the same for others.
>
> (Tarn Bright, Safe Families/Home for Good)

111. Joshua 2:1-21, 6:17-25; Matthew 1:5; Hebrews 11:31; James 2:25.
112. https://safefamilies.uk/https://homeforgood.org.uk/ (accessed 17.11.25).

What is especially interesting in the way that Rahab joins in (is 'missioned' to by the spies who are sent out by Joshua) is that this is exactly the kind of mission that Jesus sends his 'spies' out on in Luke 10:5-9. Jesus says accept hospitality and kindness, preach, heal and proclaim a blessing of peace on the household. This kind of mission bears fruit.

Just as welcome and hospitality are at the heart of how we are together in fellowship, so too is this at the heart of our outward mission. Even Moses, on the run, full of guilt and with mission the last thing on his mind, stumbles across a well, defends some sisters, draws water for their flocks, and ends up marrying one of them in Exodus 2:15-22. He is doing the kind of shepherding he does later with Israel, protecting, providing, giving water. He is also unknowingly prefiguring the Good Shepherd, Jesus, who gave the same access to living water at the Samaritan well many years later in John 4. Both Moses and Jesus are invited to stay. This Midianite family becomes part of the Israelite story as does the woman at the well and her Samaritan village. Loving our neighbour is always personal, always caring, always sacrificial and always offering the water of life. Usually there is a divide to cross – where fear and uncertainty may prevent us from engaging with our neighbour – or pride and self-centredness mean that we don't see them as Jesus sees them. But what starts with a relatively small act

> In recent years I have been discovering the power and freedom of seeking to pay attention to God right in the ordinary moments of life – using everyday activities as a prompt to intentionally reorientate my heart, and in so doing to experience more fully the activity and presence of God in and around me.
>
> (Katharine Hill, Care for the Family)

of kindness can grow into the transformation of a whole city or region. As we saw in Part 3, the invitation for foreigners to join in with worship and feasting is the beginning of Israel's mission to the world.

> [He] loves the foreigner residing among you, giving them food and clothing. And you are to love those who are foreigners, for you yourselves were foreigners in Egypt.
>
> (Deuteronomy 10:18-19)

The Apostle Paul described the vision of God for Israel's purpose like this:

> Understand, then, that those who have faith are children of Abraham. Scripture foresaw that God would justify the Gentiles by faith, and announced the gospel in advance to Abraham: 'All nations will be blessed through you.' So those who rely on faith are blessed along with Abraham, the man of faith.
>
> (Galatians 3:7-9)

and:

> This mystery is that through the gospel the Gentiles are heirs together with Israel, members together of one body, and sharers together in the promise in Christ Jesus.
>
> (Ephesians 3:6)

Looking out, sent by Jesus, in Mark's Gospel

In his book *Practicing the Way*, John Mark Comer defines Jesus' ministry in three categories:

Making space for the gospel (i.e. hospitality), Preaching the gospel (i.e. proclamation) and Demonstrating the gospel.[113]

113. Comer, *Practicing the Way*, pp. 142-168.

The late Roger Forster, church leader and Bible teacher, used the phrase 'Words, Works and Wonders': Words (Good news for the poor), Works (binding up broken hearts), and Wonders (Release for the captives).[114]

How about we combine these definitions into:

> Welcome (Compassionate Expression: hospitality, eating together, sharing space and activity),
>
> Words (Articulate Expression: preaching, teaching, writing, art and storytelling);
>
> Works (Practical Expression: acts of kindness, justice, compassion, and restoration);
>
> Wonders (Supernatural Expression: miracles, healing, deliverance, prophecy, supernatural gifts and surprising results).

I believe the mission for a disciple of Jesus is to be a tour guide to the kingdom. How freeing it is to know that although we are commissioned to share and be Jesus to those around us, it is not on us to make decisions for others, we can only signpost people towards Jesus. To be a tour guide we need to know where we are going. We need knowledge of the destination and the attraction and engaging along the journey. So, our responsibility is to stay immersed in the word, infectious with our faith and remain close to Jesus.

(Marie Aitken, Hillsong UK)

114. FORSTER, ROGER. 'Ichthus Christian Fellowship, London.' *Transformation 9, no. 2* (1992): 15–23, www.jstor.org/stable/43052358 (accessed 3.11.25).

The aim of this mission is both to bring the kingdom of heaven to the earth now – to invite the rule and reign of Jesus into our present reality – and also to point the way towards this eternal life continuing and growing into the future. The future vision we find in the Bible – a new heaven and a new earth, God living among his people, 'no more death or mourning or crying or pain' (Revelation 21:1-4) is what is declared. Jesus inaugurated this when he lived on the earth, and the Church continues to demonstrate it, and also proclaims that one day this hope for peace, salvation, the end of evil and everything made new will be totally fulfilled. Our welcome, words, works and wonders point towards this by also giving a foretaste of this: let your kingdom come and your will be done, on earth as it is in heaven, now and forevermore.

What does my mission look like? Trying not just to be nice, but to point people to Jesus in words and action. Helping my neighbour with technical issues and eating meals with her – she is eighty-one and lives alone. On the surface, she isn't someone who I'd naturally hang out with or perhaps offer me anything to progress my work or social skills but that's okay because I can show her love through time, cooking and help. Approaching someone on the street and asking, 'if God could answer a prayer for you, what would it be?' – and being able to pray that person's prayer and ask if he had faith. Speaking to my barber gym instructor, delivery driver and my physio in a short period of time and just asking them if they had faith and inviting them to church.

(Nicky Wong, All Hallows Church, Bow)

Welcome

In Mark's Gospel we can see Jesus showing love for his neighbours in all these ways. We have seen how often he welcomes strangers into his house. His hospitality extends to thousands of people. He makes space for children, even taking them in his arms. He stops what he is doing and makes room for an embarrassed woman, and for a shunned blind man. He allows himself to be found and interrupted by a foreign woman whose daughter is demonised. He lets his own personal space be invaded as people press into him. In the last week of his life he has a meal with a leper and a woman who anoints him and he prepares a meal for his disciples.[115] Making space with his time, his home, and even his reputation characterises the way that Jesus treats people. This is good news for all of them. Jesus is not precious about these resources he has. He is unhurried, unafraid and unembarrassed. And as a result, people follow him.

Welcome and hospitality is a very strong theme in the Bible – both when it is done well and also when the opposite happens with terror and violation. Today, our welcome to others – ideally not done begrudgingly but with sacrificial openness – can be so countercultural that it is the most evangelistic act imaginable. I have always admired the work of Rob Parsons through the organisation Care for the Family.[116] What I hadn't realised, until his book *A Knock at the Door*[117] was published, was that he and his wife, Dianne, had opened their home to a homeless man, Ronnie, who then became part of their household for the next forty-five years. Now I know why Rob has been so effective in his ministry; why his words have integrity and authority. This is true welcome, one that offers

115. Mark 6:32-44; 8:1-10; Mark 10:13-16; 5:30-33; Mark 10:48-52; Mark 7:24-30; Mark 3:10; 5:31; Mark 14:3-31.
116. www.careforthefamily.org.uk/ (accessed 3.11.25).
117. Rob Parsons, *A Knock at the Door* (London: William Collins, 2024).

good news but also invites good news as it is reciprocated and then mutually shared.

Going the extra mile (as Jesus would say . . .) is the premise of the popular book, *Unreasonable Hospitality*, by Will Guidara, whose subtitle is: 'The remarkable power of giving people more than they expect'.[118] It has stories from the hospitality industry of surprising kindness that wins over guests – leading both to their satisfaction as well as the restaurant's success. The knowledge of the power of an 'over-welcome' is not new. Down the centuries this has been one of the most significant gifts of the Church to its neighbours. The monastic movements of Europe, as the Church was being formally formed through the Middle Ages, and up to today, may be thought of primarily as places of prayer and study, closed communities of saints, but in fact they were centres of hospitality. Chapter 53 of the Rule of St Benedict[119] (who lived in the fifth and sixth century) is dedicated to hospitality and looking after the poor and opens with the line: 'All guests who arrive should be received as if they were Christ.' In churches today this is seen in welcoming and warm spaces, food banks, fostering and adoption, Alpha meals, Street Pastors,[120] lunches for the elderly

> Do the simple things often, even if you are not very good at them. I have found the simple teachings the hardest of all to do e.g. love and serve others, forgive and seek forgiveness, consider others, be kind, generous, faithful, patient etc. Similarly with prayer, I hold onto the teaching of keep it simple, keep it honest and keep it going!
>
> (Robin Vincent, Care for the Family)

118. Will Guidara, *Unreasonable Hospitality* (London: Ebury Edge, 2024).
119. Published: New York: St Martin's Essentials, 2021.
120. www.streetpastors.org/ (accessed 3.11.25).

and the welcome and care given to refugees and asylum seekers. And of course, in every informal and personal act of hospitality done by followers of Jesus: from Mary and Martha of Bethany to Rob and Dianne Parsons, to every cup of water given in Jesus' name.

Words

'Son, your sins are forgiven' (Mark 2:5) and 'Daughter, your faith has healed you. Go in peace and be freed from your suffering' (Mark 5:34) are beautiful, simple and intimate words to hear. Jesus' words may intrigue, challenge, explain or bring direct revelation. He does not speak in parables to make his teaching easier but so that people will have to use their heart, soul, mind and strength to understand – and as they do that, they will either submit to or resist the truth. But at times he explains and prophesies so that there is a directness and clarity which is helpfully unavoidable. The disciples have parables explained. The rich young ruler is challenged over his money.[121] Whatever his words are – parables, commands, prophecies,

> I have tried to practise the art of being interrupted. Yesterday I was racing to get a tube train but ended up bumping into three different individuals. Each one had something either on their mind or dealing with. With each I paused to pray with them. I arrived late to the meeting but had seen God touching lives by praying with someone in the moment they needed it.
>
> (Cris Rogers, Spring Harvest, All Hallows Church Bow, Making Disciples)

121. Mark 4:10-12,34; Mark 10:17-25.

teaching about how to live life in the kingdom, here on the earth – people are amazed.

> The people were all so amazed that they asked each other, 'What is this? A new teaching – and with authority! He even gives orders to impure spirits and they obey him.' News about him spread quickly over the whole region of Galilee.
>
> (Mark 1:27-28)

How about that for the impact of words! These kinds of words persuaded people to give up everything and follow him. They brought Lazarus and a little girl to life. To bring someone to life through our words is such a privilege. When we share our own stories and experience about the love of God, we are witnesses to the power of Jesus. Our words become like Jesus' own words, bringing an invitation to life and a conviction to turn away from death.

Words are very powerful today. Emails and texts are powerful; tweets are powerful; speeches are powerful; rallying cries are powerful; slogans are powerful. In our sophisticated society, words still have spiritual power to build up or destroy. Proverbs 18:21 says that 'The tongue has the power of life and death', and the book of James highlights the potential violence directed through the 'rudder' of the tongue (3:4). The evidence of this in social media, inciting speech, mockery, and the mix of religious language with racist, arrogant and oppressive talk is all around us. But the gift of the gift of prophecy, to encourage, comfort and build up – words that are gentle, wise, gracious and godly – is the most amazing supernatural resource for effective preaching, writing, explaining and insight. Therefore, we can adopt whatever means we have – using our phones, mics, keyboards and cameras – to speak life and see what was bitter turn sweet, and what was dead come alive.

Works

Welcome, words, works and wonders all seem to blend into one another. In Peter's sermon in Acts 10:38, he sums up Jesus as going round 'doing good and healing all who were under the power of the devil'. Good works come about when he is seen stretching himself out for others. The feeding of the thousands is a welcome, a miracle, and is certainly a good work for so many hungry people. The phrase good deeds – literally 'beautiful works' – is often used as an encouragement and even as a command in the epistles. There is a beauty to the way Jesus sensitively restores Jairus and his wife to their now living daughter in Mark 5:40-43. He holds the hand of this little girl as she comes back to life, and holds the hand of Peter's mother-in-law as she is being healed, in Mark 1:31. He touches the hand of the man with leprosy and the man is cleansed (Mark 1:41). The kind and courageous touch of Jesus heals these people physically but also demonstrates compassion, restoration into the community, respect and love. It is beautiful when one human reaches out to touch another in respectful love.

> Over the past twenty years, I've led a ministry that supports people through some of the most painful and complex issues in life – mental health struggles, trauma, addiction, grief. I've seen how the truth of the gospel and the power of practical discipleship can transform not only individuals, but families, churches, and whole communities. Living for Jesus in my world looks like creating safe spaces where people can encounter His grace, His healing and discover his purpose for their lives.
>
> (Arianna Walker, Mercy Ministries)

Jesus' works are as powerful politically as they are intimately sensitive. In the temple he sees the way that people are being prevented from prayer and worship because of the need to pay extortionate rates to be able to join in. He turns over the tables of the moneychangers and then curses a fig tree to show how this corrupt and exclusive temple system will collapse, in Mark 11:12-21. He faces a horde of demons in order to free a totally oppressed and isolated man – and in the process he brings freedom to a region that is impacted by the uncleanness of the powers of Rome. Ched Myers, in his commentary on Mark, *Binding the Strong Man*,[122] sees Jesus' ministry as a massive political and spiritual challenge to the human and demonic powers that dominate society. In the first half of the book of Mark, Jesus confronts Jewish powers – among the authorities in the synagogues, through healings and feedings and even against demonic powers. He also does the same but further afield in the more gentile areas – addressing Roman military authority in Legion, and similarly with healings and feedings. The very middle point of the book Peter calls Jesus 'the Messiah' (Mark 8:27-30). The Messiah is the rescuer. He is the one whose good works will overturn oppressive rule and injustice. The second half of the book shows Jesus once again facing angry Jewish and Roman authorities, proclaiming a

> Seize the opportunity! In Acts 3:12 it says people saw his opportunity and addressed the crowd, we all have people we can invest in, work colleagues, friends, family, who know that you are representing Jesus and you might be the only bible people read.
>
> (Dan Hargreaves, Alive Church Lincoln)

122. Myers, *Binding the Strong Man.*

new order and confronting violence with effective, patient peace. The most beautiful deed of Jesus is his death in the cross. This is what he mentions to his friends, with increasing clarity and urgency.

> He then began to teach them that the Son of Man must suffer many things and be rejected by the elders, the chief priests and the teachers of the law, and that he must be killed and after three days rise again.
>
> (Mark 8:31)

The Son of Man, the new Adam, the perfect human who lives a life doing good, suffers and is killed. The power of goodness is not in its dominance or swinging popularity but in the secretly small nature of a seed that does its work in the hidden place and then sprouts, grows, multiplies and cannot be resisted.[123] Therefore our own good works may not look much but if they express the beauty of Jesus' kindness and the authority of his new-kingdom justice, then they will produce a harvest.

Each of us is probably not far from a Christian community that is engaged in very beautiful works. Often these are works of hospitality, as mentioned above. Healthcare today is such an imitation of the works of Jesus. Also, creating environments of beauty, protecting our natural world and addressing the causes and symptoms of climate change is both prophetic and practical. It is a good work to be in politics and government, to bring about or maintain justice and righteousness in how society functions. The education of children has often been a mark of good Christian works. Business done well – creating wealth for all, addressing poverty, making room for creativity and innovation, providing fairness and satisfying work – is an excellent way of extending the kingdom of Jesus. Throughout

123. Mark 4:26-32.

history – whether it is the monastic movements like the Cistercians of the twelfth century or Christian entrepreneurs like Cadbury, Roundtree, Colegate, Heinz, Kraft and Thomas Cook – faith in Jesus has led to excellent and fruitful workplace environments. Campaigning for social justice and engaging in social action are a continuation of the prophetic call in both the Hebrew Bible and New Testament to restore beauty through the right exercise of power. This is the good news of Jesus, once again incarnated in and through his community.

Wonders

The wonders of Jesus are very evident in Mark's Gospel. The story is full of action, power and surprise. Hardly a paragraph goes by without something inexplicable happening. Words like 'amazed' and 'astonished' crop up frequently. The healings are

> I have eighty-five houses on my street with about 230 people. I know 180 of their names and pray a blessing early every morning as I walk my dog past each house. I try to action each 'random' thought when someone comes to mind and send them a WhatsApp encouragement message, sometimes with spectacular results. One time, I sent an audio message to a guy I hadn't seen in six years, saying I was praying for his wife and children by name. He had been separated from her for over a year, but was so moved that he passed on my message and her reply was: 'Well maybe there is still hope . . .' Shortly thereafter he messaged me and said that he was back in the family home!
>
> (Simon Guillebaud, Speaker and Author, Great Lakes Outreach, Burundi)

extraordinary. Jesus speaks a word, reaches out, takes a hand, allows a touch, or declares that it is done – even somewhere else – and the healing happens! He sets people free by casting out demons. Many of the healed and delivered people then want to follow Jesus and join in with him. Their lives are so totally changed that they cannot help shouting about it to others. Bartimaeus, the man called Legion, the deaf man in Decapolis are good examples of changed lives who then go on to join Jesus or help change others' lives. The feeding of the 5,000 is miraculous but it is hard to know exactly where or when the miracle took place during that event. Was it in Jesus handing out the food, or in the disciples' hands, or in the sudden appearance of a massive pile of fish? He kept giving out the bread and divided up the two fish. Read Mark 6:33-44 and see if you can determine exactly how it took place!

His wonders are so impactful that even his disciples become afraid. He calms the storm when they are heading to Decapolis: 'They were terrified and asked each other, "Who is this? Even the wind and the waves obey him!"' (Mark 4:41). Then when Jesus arrives, he delivers a man from a legion of demons: 'Then the people began to plead with Jesus to leave their region' (Mark 5:17). A man in a synagogue has his shrivelled hand healed when Jesus tells him to stretch it out. These wonders bring so much healing, peace and rescue

> Discipleship means being courageous in our everyday life and letting Christ's love echo through our decisions, our families, and our workplaces. It means being accountable, rooted in Scripture, and willing to stand for truth and stand against injustice – even when it costs.
>
> (Warren Evans, Sports Chaplaincy UK)

to those who need it, and yet there is also a reaction of fear and anger. 'Then the Pharisees went out and began to plot with the Herodians how they might kill Jesus' (Mark 3:6). Jesus clearly finds this frustrating, but it does not stop him from declaring and enacting the supernatural power of God for a broken and hurting world. This power stirs up whatever resistance there is to the love of God, whether that is pride, resentment, or fear. It is this wonderful and triumphant power that is shown in his death:

> When you were dead in your sins and in the uncircumcision of your flesh, God made you alive with Christ. He forgave us all our sins, having cancelled the charge of our legal indebtedness, which stood against us and condemned us; he has taken it away, nailing it to the cross. And having disarmed the powers and authorities, he made a public spectacle of them, triumphing over them by the cross.
>
> (Colossians 2:13-15)

There is no shortage of the wonders of Jesus today. Our mindset, which has become increasingly human reason-focused does not readily see the supernatural work of the Spirit, or make room for him. There are places across the world where there is more eagerness and a culture of faith, where it seems that there are more wonders and miracles. The reality that prayers are not always answered in the supernatural ways we would most want also means that in our disappointment we are less inclined to imitate Jesus in his ministry of wonders. I am struck by the faith of the early Church, who in the face of persecution, disaster and cruelty, continued to pray for the sick and for surprising breakthroughs of spiritual power. They were able to live in the tension of knowing miracles and living with obstacles. The right approach is to look for the work of God – often in what we call coincidences – where we begin to see the tapestry of prayer and divine working in myriads of small and seemingly impossible ways. This then builds faith and passion to pray and speak boldly, and to allow the creative power of Jesus to work through us as we dare to live by faith.

Journeying outwards

Just as Moses' teaching in Deuteronomy was to push Israel out from their wilderness wanderings and into contact with people and places where they could live out the new community, so too the mission of Jesus in Mark's Gospel is all about being sent. He begins at home but doesn't stay there, even though it is all very exciting. He says to his friends: 'Let us go somewhere else – to the nearby villages – so I can preach there also. That is why I have come' (Mark 1:38). So he spends time between various Galilee villages and home. He then stretches out to the more gentile areas such as the Decapolis, before returning home. Then he is out again as far as Tyre, Decapolis once more, and the new Roman city of Caesarea Philippi. Again, he comes back home, then to Judea beyond the Jordan, and finally he makes his way to Jerusalem.

Jesus goes to those who are his neighbours – those that are near him and are quite like him in the way they live their lives. He also goes to others who speak his language but are further away – maybe because of distance, or because they are somewhat hidden due to their needs or the way they are treated by others.

> Being a disciple is about following Jesus, regularly asking myself the question, 'what would Jesus do right now?', and responding accordingly *in his power* – I don't succeed all the time!
>
> (Alexandra Huggins, Faith in Later Life)

He also goes to people who are easily within reach but who have a different culture, who dress differently, and have a different approach to life. And, of course, he then sends his disciples to all these groups as well as to the ends of the earth – to faraway people with faraway cultures and lifestyles.

The impetus in Mark's Gospel is always outwards, in ever increasing circles, with ever increasing impact. Even on the last day of his life, Jesus faces the high priest and the Sanhedrin; and we know that religious leaders Joseph and Nicodemus become followers.[124] He faces Pilate, the representative of Rome and world power; an empire that his followers will later turn upside down with the gospel. He is cruelly tortured by the soldiers; one of whom then worships him on the cross.[125] He meets Simon of Cyrene, father of two Gentile sons, who carries the cross (unlike the other Simon, the fisherman, who runs away), and ironically is pressed into becoming a disciple. Jesus is crucified between two thieves; one of whom is repentant and invited by Jesus into paradise in Luke 23:43. He is watched by the women disciples who have not deserted him and who are the ones who carry the first gospel message of resurrection in Luke 24:9-10.

Even being questioned and tortured, Jesus is living as a sent one.

Even hanging on the cross, Jesus is sent to redeem sinners and attract those who will worship him.

And even as Jesus dies, he is sent to those women who are watching, whose hearts are made ready to preach the good news of resurrection and new life.

124. John 19:38-39.
125. Mark 15:39.

Living Room

Looking out is all about the conviction that every human being needs Jesus! Meeting Jesus is the best thing for everyone – whatever nation they are from, or cultural background. Meeting Jesus changes everything – which is not surprising since he is the creator and restorer of all things.[126] An encounter with Jesus changes someone's heart and this fundamental spiritual change then affects everything: behaviour, purpose, identity and relationships. On the broadest level, a transformed heart impacts economics, politics, injustice, conflict, culture and family. So, it is not only good news for an individual – eternal life, and with it, transformative power now – but it is Jesus' way of bringing justice, peace and joy into every part of humanity and creation. God's big plan was 'through him [Jesus] to reconcile to himself all things, whether things on earth or things in heaven, by making peace through his blood, shed on the cross' (Colossians 1:20).

In view of such a significant mission, the outward dimension of being a follower of Jesus can be a challenge. Atrophy is where something or someone becomes, over time, less vigorous or effective because of a lack of use. Those forty years of going in circles did that to Israel (apart from Joshua and Caleb). Jesus, however, shows how to live with vigour by serving, caring and witnessing to the love of God to everyone around him.

> I love inspiring hope in those who feel lost, reminding them that the Lord has a purpose and a good plan for their lives. Shifting my focus to others fills me with purpose and keeps my heart open.
>
> (John O'Connor, Junction 42)

126. Colossians 1:16,20; Acts 3:21

Churches that do not have an outward focus have a tendency to shrink quite rapidly – especially now that membership of a church is no longer a culturally expected norm. The irony is that it takes a fair amount of time and resource to simply keep a church open for worship and for fellowship, let alone any sense of purposeful mission. Of course, we need to prioritise our rhythms of prayer and worship and also ensure that we have a life-filled community into which we can invite people. But somehow doing this as urgent and important before the 'luxury' of our mission can mean we never get round to an outward focus. Also, it is easier and safer to attend to our religious duties and church family affairs than take the risks of declaring God's love to others who may ignore us or even oppose us.

The example of Jesus, however, shows that the outward mission of loving our neighbours is as life-giving and spiritually forming as the other spiritual practices we engage in. Loving beyond is integral to being a disciple rather than the optional extra once we get everything else in place. Our worship of God *is* our serving of others. The way we work together to display God's love to a broken world *is* our fellowship life. And to see it from the opposite angle, worship and prayer is extraordinarily evangelistic. It is a shame if there is no one who does not know Jesus experiencing his presence in our midst. Good community life is a gift for those who are isolated and lonely. It is only ever tested or even enjoyed properly when there are new people being invited in.

Worship leads to being transformed which then leads to bringing transformation

How might we then attend to our hearts so that they are orientated outwards, and what can we learn from Moses and Jesus about the nature of mission-shaped discipleship? There is a pattern throughout the Bible of personal transformation that leads to community and society transformation. It is especially seen in the call of the prophets; those whose hearts are shaped by God's message who therefore intentionally shape the world around them according to the nature and power of the kingdom of heaven.

Isaiah's experience of an encounter with God as he worships in the temple in Isaiah 6 leads to the call to mission. Integral in this mission is his continued worship life – he is a great worshipper and songwriter. He is also committed to family and appears to have developed a circle of disciples. Isaiah is best known for his mission to declare the justice of God to complacent and rich religious people, as well as engaging with the kings of his day over the bigger political issues. All this came with the announcement of the coming of Jesus and his kingdom – faith in Jesus drives the call for justice, repentance and love.

> A lifestyle of worship – an aim that ALL that I do can bring thanks and praise to God, whilst remembering that when I mess up I have a God who is looking to forgive, encourage and provide the next opportunity for me to learn and grow.
>
> When life is lived out this way, I believe it stands out to those around you and enables a foundation of honesty and integrity upon which others enquire of Jesus. This often looks like friends or colleagues coming to you with difficult life issues or asking if you will pray about something for them.
>
> (Peter Wilson, Spring Harvest, Physiotherapist)

Saul/Paul had a similar call to mission. Beginning with a powerful experience of repentance and worship, he is then invited into loving Christian community where he is graciously forgiven and respected. His heartfelt devotion to Jesus and his brothers and sisters drives his mission of carrying the gospel to the Gentiles. It is clear that Paul's mission is part of his worship of Jesus, and it is the natural shape of fellowship life for him.

This pattern is common throughout the Bible. Abraham, Isaac and Jacob have intense encounters with God in worship where they then hear the call to follow the Lord.[127] Gideon's call starts with worship, moves into family life and then results in outward driven action.[128] Elisha is drawn into friendship, worships God, joins in with many other prophets and follows the call to bring healing, speak truth to power, care for the poor and influence politics.[129]

> I try to live in a way that's consistent whether I'm on a platform or at the park with my little girl. For me, it looks like giving time to people, offering encouragement even when I'm tired, choosing to do the right thing when no one's watching. At home we sing and pray with our little girl, we speak openly about Jesus, and we try to create a culture of grace where it's OK to mess up. We have a great church community and friends who really know us. That's important!
>
> (Philippa Hanna, Singer Songwriter)

127. Genesis 12:7-9; Genesis 26:23-25; Genesis 28:10-22.
128. Judges 6:11-24.
129. 1 Kings 19:19-21; 2 Kings 2:9-15.

Worship is God's gift to us, to open our eyes and ears to who he is and who we are in Christ. It is the place of activation of our outward mission; of conviction, or a stirring of a holy discontent where we so feel God's justice and love that we are compelled to give our lives to serve his purposes in bringing restoration. Every time we eat the bread and drink the cup,[130] we recall the sacrifice of Jesus and surely that moves us to extend that sacrifice further. The Israelites remembered their redemption from Egypt by worshipping, praying, telling the story, reading the sticky notes on the doorposts and so springing into a life of action. Even a weekly worship time with others in church is a great rhythm where we can follow these prophets' own experience: to hear from God and to go once more into his world with his Word. This is a good reason to go to church on a Sunday! It means that every week we can reset our sails; receive instructions on who to serve, how to live and what choices to make.

Habits of service, giving and generosity

Even our outward focus can be strengthened and fruitful with habitual attitudes and practices. According to Dallas Willard in *Spirit of the Disciplines*, our serving may often be an overflow of love, our act of witness freely given from a thankful heart. But it may also act as a discipline to help train ourselves away from superiority.[131] Serving others is the way of the cross. To become lower than someone else, to wash their feet, to carry their load, not only helps them, but also it helps to free us from pride, arrogance and resentment. Therefore, our outward focus is both a part of our inward formation as well as a part of our mission to the world. It is this very spirit of challenging humility, as we engage in serving and giving, that is in itself

130. See 1 Corinthians 11:26.
131. Willard, *Spirit of the Disciplines*, pp. 188-191.

a prophetic sign to a world that longs for this kind of free and unfettered love. When a disciple is seen to be generous and humble, this is provocative. Although some are repelled by Christ in us, many others would like this kind of heart for themselves.

Similarly, giving, along with frugality, secrecy and sacrifice, are disciplines that help us, as well as helping others beyond us. We do good – but without any desire for reward or praise – and in this, others are blessed by our actions or generosity, while we too find ourselves closer to God. Thomas à Kempis who produced the devotional book *The Imitation of Christ* in the fifteenth century, wrote: 'He that seeks no outward witness for himself, it appeared openly that he hath committed himself wholly to God.'[132] When we give, we are contributing to the needs of others but also towards our own simplicity of life and reliance on the provision of God. The discipline of giving then sets off a chain reaction of thankfulness, needs met, praise, trust and gospel fruitfulness. It is explosive in its effect, spreading the love of God deep, far and wide.

> Working for an organisation like Youth for Christ[133] and volunteering in the youth-work at my church feel like obvious examples of how I live for Jesus in my world. However, what underpins everything in my life whether it's my work and ministry, or my friendships and my hobbies, is my hope to try and bring a little more of Jesus' love, joy and creativity to the world. No matter the space, place or people, I believe this is the root behind anything I do.
>
> (Bethan Newman, Youth for Christ)

132. Thomas à Kempis, *The Imitation of Christ* (London: Penguin Classics, 2005), p. 177.
133. https://yfc.co.uk/ (accessed 6.11.25).

> This service that you perform is not only supplying the needs of the Lord's people but is also overflowing in many expressions of thanks to God. Because of the service by which you have proved yourselves, others will praise God for the obedience that accompanies your confession of the gospel of Christ, and for your generosity in sharing with them and with everyone else.
>
> (2 Corinthians 9:12-13)

Bearing in mind that outward disciplines are good for our hearts and good for others, it is the most obvious thing that we should copy Jesus by giving, serving, living simply and looking at the world through his eyes. Everyone is a winner when we empty ourselves and give ourselves away.

Everything is included in the mission

Most of us only have 168 hours in our week. Much of that may be at work or with household/family, and a fair amount is sleeping. We're obviously trying to put in some prayer, Bible reading and meditation into that mix, joining in with church, small group, rota-filling etc. Which leaves only a bit for street evangelism and signs and wonders down the High Street. Quite frankly, there's not a lot of time for direct outward witness and mission.

> Jesus invites us to 'follow him', therefore, our everyday life, should be marked by a desire to see where He is at work, to stay close and walk in his ways. To be a disciple is someone who points others to Jesus.
>
> (Damian Wharton, Scripture Union Northern Ireland)

The good news is that an outward facing life is not just about classic Christian ministry activities – it is a whole life attitude, belief and approach. Of course, we are called to be focused in living for Jesus, taking every opportunity to share his love and life with those around us. Sometimes, however, we turn witness into an activity that is so separate from our everyday lives that we miss the example of Jesus who sanctified everything he touched, and embodied whole-life mission rather than making it an add-on to his every-day. In Revelation 21:5 Jesus says, 'I am making everything new!' Everything! He blesses and transforms everything, and everything is in his sights for holiness and redemption. Justice and righteousness; Spiritual freedom; Acts of mercy; Creation care; New community; Beauty. And much of Jesus' time on earth addressing these things is done outside of his day job of rabbinical-style teaching. He is at home or in someone else's house for a meal when he brings healing, release and peace. He is strolling by the beach when he transforms a struggling fishing business from an overnight failure to a morning success.

He changes the fortunes of every poor and swindled person in the city of Jericho while having tea with Zaccheus. It is often when he is between jobs that these missional encounters take place – in the market and on the road. And rather than an evangelistic stadium campaign with the piano playing chords, Jesus even kicks off his whole ministry at a local wedding by making a lot of new wine for the groom's parents.[134]

The gospel of the kingdom of heaven is not a narrow gospel offering a quick route to the afterlife. It is the original plan of God in Genesis, renewed and re-embodied by Jesus. Humans are called to rule and subdue the earth. That is to bring order, to gather, to catalogue, to judge, to name, to place, to discover

134. See Luke 19; John 2.

and to celebrate. It is to add creative pressure and make and mould and fashion and design and engineer. All this has been twisted in so many ways into oppression, submission, hoarding and selfish domination since the fall of humankind even though we still all enjoy the glimpses of its beauty and glory when we find ourselves living as humans made in the image of God. Humans are also called to cultivate and keep. We explored these words *abad* and *shamar* in the context of worship, noting that they are first found in God's command given to humanity in Genesis 2 to look after the earth. That is to serve, dress, work and bring to flourishing all that has been given to us by God. It is to protect, guard, attend to, preserve and keep. We are called to nurture life, to cherish and love what we have been given, to bring out the best in it and to search it out so that its beauty can be seen and enjoyed. Once again, the Fall turned this into sweat and toil, into imprisonment, lockdown, trampling and battle. The good news of the kingdom is that we proclaim freedom to all that is oppressed and release to all that is held captive. This includes people and planet, animals,

> At ROC, being a disciple looks like faith in action – loving people where they are, whether that's on a late-night street patrol, mentoring a young person, or simply being a listening ear at a ROC Chat hub helping people with a mental health crisis. It's not just about words – it's about presence, compassion, and community restoration.
>
> Being a disciple means choosing kindness, stepping into brokenness with hope, and helping others find their own strength. It's the small, consistent acts of love that make a big difference.
>
> (Debra Green, Redeeming Our Communities)

plants and the whole of creation. The work of A Rocha,[135] for instance, equips us to live out that first mandate to cultivate and keep the gift of God's earth. A Rocha works with churches, land managers, environmental leaders and individuals and families to educate, inspire and address the call to humanity to look after the earth, bring climate stability and health and shalom to the natural world, and in so doing to see the fullness of the gospel of the kingdom of heaven – natural and spiritual – expressed on earth.

This gospel is a declaration of *shalom* for the earth, family, business, bodies, governments, science, engineering and all the arts. Because of the breadth of this gospel, we can live it out wherever we are and whatever context we are in. There is no part of our lives and this world that should be untouched by the grace, healing and justice of Jesus. The outward dimension of being a disciple must include politics and the environment. It will address education and healthcare, our social interactions, legal systems and businesses. Media, the arts, recreation and sport are all being made new by Jesus and require his followers to encounter him, be changed by him, filled with his Spirit and then live within all these spheres of life in such a way that heaven's rule is experienced on earth. Therefore, we can imitate Jesus, the Creator of the universe, in the way we make food, play music, grow tomatoes and play football. When everything we do is in praise of God, then the power of heaven coming to earth will affect what we say, how we spend our time and money, our bodies, friendships, witness – all our work, rest and play. This is probably more demanding than setting aside some time for evangelistic witness occasionally. It is certainly not saying that everything we do is automatically pointing to the kingdom – we are too often lazy, unfocused and even irreverent in many of our daily activities.

135. https://arocha.org.uk/about-us/who-we-are/ (accessed 3.11.25).

But what if we saw them through the eyes of Jesus, and began to delight in the possibility of our whole lives becoming a holy and prophetic praise to God?

What we do does not have to be obviously Christian to become holy. Bread, fish and wine were all multiplied and made delicious in the hands of Jesus.

We can bear the fruit of the Spirit in every activity and this will bless those around us.

Our witness of welcome, words, works and wonders – fuelled by the gifts of the Spirit[136] - will then be evident in all kinds of ordinary and extraordinary situations.

Being sent by Jesus, out of our comfort zone, walking by faith, healing the sick, and proclaiming the kingdom is the most awesome way to live.

Made in the image of God – ruling, subduing, cultivating, and keeping – is the way we were designed to be. It is now a prophetic sign of all that Jesus is making new.

We continue to reign in this contested Kingdom as we subdue with care and rule with wisdom.

Our care for the planet and its inhabitants can be characterised by our serving and protection.

> Being a disciple is to care more about what Jesus thinks than what others think.
>
> (Rob Parsons, Care for the Family)

136. 1 Corinthians 12.

We can fill the earth with what we have formed and built, using justice and compassion.

Our creativity displays the ingenuity and artistry of God.

Now is not the time to ignore these God commands in order to avoid the traps and mires of strife and selfishness. Instead, our worship of God is beautifully displayed in what we do, how we do it and for whom we do it. To all teachers, medics, artists, engineers, farmers, administrators, managers, athletes and dog groomers: there is a stunningly beautiful city to be built.[137]

Out to the world: A story

Many years ago we had a speaker at our church who prophesied that the church would be known for its hospitality. I remember church meetings where people had said sadly that they had not found much kindness from each other, let alone give it to others outside the church! So we first had to learn how to extend hospitality and trust with one another as a fellowship. Nevertheless, there was a desire to somehow connect with the community in a way that hadn't been tried before. At that time the church was challenged financially and so was looking to see how renting out the rooms of the church's new building could help cover costs. We ended up with lots of bookings from our local authorities and health services. They kept re-booking because the welcome was warm and the food was so nice. As well as being full of people wearing lanyards, the building was also now open for those who were struggling with life controlling issues and pressures that were affecting them financially and socially. We wanted to extend this latter ministry of hospitality and care to another housing estate, and so my wife, Bev, and others ended up praying round an old rent

137. Martin J. Young, *This is That: How to See the Kingdom of Heaven in Everyday Living* (Welwyn Garden City: Malcolm Down Publishing, 2021).

office. A week later, at a regional health authority conference hosted in the church centre, we were asked whether would be able to take on that very building to do some of the kinds of things we were doing in the church – and it would be entirely funded! Although the funding didn't last many years, that initiative led to the of a charity, the social action arm of the church, which recently won the King's Award for its work across the borough in food banks, furniture provision, advice and guidance, DIY help and elderly care. That old rent office is now the base for a church plant, as well as offering hospitality and care in the community. We then started a church in another town, with the same aims of welcome and support, and found an old community centre to operate from. After this we were asked to operate the local library, and because of that going well were approached to run a youth and community centre with playing fields in yet another town. We had already planted a church there a few years before and were in the process of looking for a hospitable place to replicate these kinds of church ministry. A deaf church began, after first having the hospitality of a deaf café run occasionally in the building, and this church is now flourishing. During Covid, because of the committed and kind work of our volunteers, the church was asked by the County Council to meet the food hunger needs in our borough, and also a neighbouring district. Along the way many new friends have been made who have become brothers and sisters in the family of God. Often these have been people who would otherwise have been overlooked, with no one to invite them to an Alpha course or to step into their lives with kindness, prayer and commitment. It has been like living in the parable of the feast, where all kinds of people get invited to sit at the table and join in with the party.[138]

138. Luke 14:15-24

This twenty-year journey started small – with desires and yearnings, constraints and challenges, and what almost seemed like a casual prophetic word. It has resulted in churches being started, buildings repurposed as places of welcome and support, and so many relationships of favour, friendship and collaboration throughout the region. You will know of many other churches and ministries with a similar story. There are some remarkable examples of the welcome, words, works and wonders of Jesus being displayed across our nation these days; those who bring expertise, faith and favour to city and national government leaders, as well as the personal encounter and touch of kindness simply and sincerely done in the name of Jesus. The upward essence of worship and prayer, and the inward practice of serving one another in the community of Jesus is exactly the right mix to outwardly bring transformation to the places where we live. The gospel begins in our own hearts and among our own relationships as a church, and cannot help but multiply and spread out its life-giving seeds of justice, peace and joy.

Artist: Ruth Hearson

Playground

For all the resources, links and information about the contributors mentioned, scan the code to visit:

www.springharvest.org/resources/no-greater-life/

Practices

Explore practices that help us be sent by Jesus. These include service, generosity, evangelism, workplace faith, politics, social justice and social action.

Resources

Mark Greene, *Fruitfulness on the Frontline* (IVP, 2014)

Paula Gooder, *The Joy of the Gospel* (London: Church House Publishing, 2015) – Study guide and course

Ruth Valerio, *L is for Lifestyle* (London: IVP, 2019)

Ruth Valerio, *Saying Yes to Life*, Ruth Valerio (London: SPCK, 2019)

https://talkingjesus.org – Research, Course, and Workbook about sharing faith

https://alpha.org.uk/ – Start or join a course

https://operationworld.org/ – How to pray for our world

Lectio Divina 4

A Radical Reset
Luke 4:17-21

Let's pause and pray with a *Lectio 365* Morning Prayer, meditating on how we can join in with God's mission today.

Together we will pray (P.R.A.Y.): P – pausing to be still, R – rejoicing with a psalm and reflecting on Scripture, A – asking God to help us and others and Y – yielding to his will in our lives.

Pause

As I enter prayer now, I pause to be still; to breathe slowly, to re-centre my scattered senses upon the presence of God.

Pause and pray

Prayer of Approach

God of rescue and restoration,
Thank you for your great and beautiful mission in the world.
Here I am, Lord,
Fill me with your Spirit and send me.

Rejoice and reflect

I choose to rejoice in God's sovereignty today, joining with the ancient praise of all God's people in the words of Psalm 29:

> The voice of the Lord twists mighty oaks
> and strips the forests bare.
> In his Temple everyone shouts, 'Glory!'
> The Lord rules over the floodwaters.
> The Lord reigns as king forever.
> The Lord gives his people strength.
> The Lord blesses them with peace.
>
> (Psalm 29:9-11, NLT)

Pause and pray

Jesus, empowered by the Spirit, is embarking on his three-year mission to announce the coming of God's kingdom. He begins in the synagogue in his home town . . .

> . . . the scroll of the prophet Isaiah was handed to him. Unrolling it, he found the place where it is written:

> 'The Spirit of the Lord is on me,
> because he has anointed me
> to proclaim good news to the poor.
> He has sent me to proclaim freedom for the prisoners
> and recovery of sight for the blind,
> to set the oppressed free,
> to proclaim the year of the Lord's favour.'
>
> Then he rolled up the scroll, gave it back to the attendant and sat down. The eyes of everyone in the synagogue were fastened on him. He began by saying to them, 'Today this scripture is fulfilled in your hearing.'
>
> (Luke 4:17-21)

In Jewish law there is a radical, society-shaping command. Every half century, God declared a Jubilee year – an economic and social reset for Israel.[139] At that time enslaved Israelites were to be liberated, and the poor could reclaim the land of their ancestors. If practised, Jubilee had the power to eliminate generational poverty and economic oppression.

It's this Jubilee dream that echoes through the Isaiah passage Jesus chose to read. With these words, Jesus announced a new Jubilee. His mission is to offer a greater freedom and restoration to Israel and others: a liberation that has the power to transform both my daily life and my eternal destiny.[140]

Ask

I find the concept of Jubilee deeply challenging in a culture shaped by materialism.

139. Leviticus 25:10-17,25-31,39-43. Passages other than Leviticus 25 talk about forty-nine years not fifty – forty-nine being seven times seven, making the Jubilee year like a special Sabbath year.
140. For more on this, read J.H. Wright, *The Mission of God* (Nottingham: IVP, 2006), p. 301.

God, is there anything I own that I would struggle to give up? Please show me which of my possessions truly possess me.

Pause and pray

I name some of the politicians, business leaders, bankers and economists that shape the economic culture of my nation.

God, help them create systems of liberation instead of oppression, of equity instead of inequality.

Pause and pray

Yield

As I return to the passage I look out for a particular word or phrase that the Holy Spirit seems to be highlighting to me today.

> . . . the scroll of the prophet Isaiah was handed to him. Unrolling it, he found the place where it is written:
>
> 'The Spirit of the Lord is on me,
> because he has anointed me
> to proclaim good news to the poor.
> He has sent me to proclaim freedom for the prisoners
> and recovery of sight for the blind,
> to set the oppressed free,
> to proclaim the year of the Lord's favour.'
>
> Then he rolled up the scroll, gave it back to the attendant and sat down. The eyes of everyone in the synagogue were fastened on him. He began by saying to them, 'Today this scripture is fulfilled in your hearing.'
>
> (Luke 4:17-21)

I take a moment to reflect on any word or phrase that the Holy Spirit is highlighting for me.

Pause

Theologian Christopher Wright notes that Isaiah's words bring 'a holistic dimension into the mission that Jesus sets out for himself'. It's not all 'flowery metaphors or spiritual allegories . . .'[141] The good news of God's kingdom brings life-changing benefits for those who are poor, imprisoned, ill or oppressed. How is Jesus inviting me into this kind of whole-life-altering mission in my community?

Pause and pray

Yielding Prayer

Jesus, show me how to join in with your work of liberation in the lives of those around me. Lead me towards greater generosity with all you've given me. Empower me to speak words of hope and eternal destiny and teach me to pray faith-filled prayers for transformation.

Yielding Promise

And now, as I prepare to take this time of prayer into the coming day, the Lord Jesus who loves me says in Matthew's Gospel:

> God authorized and commanded me to commission you: Go out and train everyone you meet, far and near, in this way of life, marking them by baptism in the threefold name: Father, Son, and Holy Spirit.
>
> (Matthew 28:18-19, *The Message*)

141. Ibid.

Closing Prayer

Father, help me to live this day to the full,
being true to you in every way.
Jesus, help me to give myself away to others,
being kind to everyone I meet.
Spirit, help me to love the lost,
proclaiming Christ in all I do and say.
Amen

Lectio 365 is a prayer app from 24-7 Prayer. Download for free to pray the Bible morning, noon and night.

Further Bible verses to read and contemplate

Deuteronomy 32:43; Romans 15:7-10,16-19;
Deuteronomy 11:22-24

Journal – pray, reflect, write

Use chapter 11 of Cris Rogers' *Making Disciples* (East Sussex: Essential Christian, 2018), pp. 48-53 as the exercise in journalling, reflecting and praying.

Reflective prayer

1 Clement 59.3 – 61.3. Clement, who became bishop in Rome, was a contemporary of some of the apostles and died in about AD99. This prayer of his is the earliest recorded Christian prayer outside of the Bible. Read and reflect.

www.biola.edu/blogs/good-book-blog/2012/a-powerful-prayer-from-clement-of-rome-apostolic-fathers-3

Action

- What mission can you do or join in with?
- Who are the people or places that Jesus is calling you to serve?
- How can your everyday life more fully reflect and amplify the goodness of God?
- What are the projects of compassion and justice that you could support, join in with and pray for?

Group Bible study

A tale of two rescues

Mark 5:1-20 and Mark 9:9-29

These are two very dramatic stories that clearly show the battle between good and evil, the grace of Jesus and the oppression of the devil.

- Notice how Jesus invades enemy territory in both stories. Talk together about how he gets to Legion and what happens on the way (4:35-41); and also how the purity and majesty of the mountain top-transfiguration is shattered (9:14-18).
- What might Mark mean by these phrases: 'Let us go over *to the other side*' (Mark 4:35, my emphasis) and 'As they were *coming down the mountain*' (Mark 9:9)?

- Notice in both stories the impure spirit and the violent and disturbing language. How spiritually oppressed or out of your depth have you have felt as a disciple?
- Why do you think Jesus asks questions of or about those who are in need of his help?
- Compare the boy's father and his faith with the disciples and their faith in chapter 9. What is said?
- Compare the man set free with the people around him in chapter 5. What is said?
- Talk together about what these stories tell us about being a disciple of Jesus today.

Wholehearted – a series of studies about the heart #4

Undivided heart

> Teach me your way, Lord,
> that I may rely on your faithfulness;
> give me an undivided heart,
> that I may fear your name.
>
> (Psalm 86:11)

An undivided heart is praised in the Bible, but what does it mean? The Hebrew word used in this verse means a heart that is joined – and yet the psalmist is not talking here about unity of many people, but the joining that happens in his own heart. Psalm 12:2 talks about those who lie, speak with flattering lips and have a double heart. This is literally written as 'heart heart' – a two-hearted person. So an undivided heart is one that does not lie nor has two agendas. Jeremiah 32:39 says, 'I will give them singleness of heart and action'. That is literally 'one' heart, and a road or way to live on. Similarly Ezekiel 11:19 says, 'I will give them an undivided heart and put a new spirit in them' – once again that is literally 'one' heart. Jeremiah 24:7 says: 'they will return to me with all their heart.'

So we see that God is looking for a unified heart, a joined-up heart, one that is not divided with double thinking, giving in to temptation or split in its loyalties. The people saw this in David and so wanted him as their king. King David's prayer for his son Solomon was for him to have a whole heart and a 'willing mind' (1 Chronicles 28:9). 'Whole' or 'wholly devoted' is the word *shalem*, is similar to *shalom*; it is where his heart would be complete, blameless and fully devoted to the things of God. Solomon prays this for the people and Hezekiah prays it for himself. It is the prayer of a good king.[142] And yet the Bible says that even Solomon lost his way and he 'turned his heart after other gods, and his heart was not fully devoted to the LORD his God, as the heart of David his father had been' (1 Kings 11:4).

It is possible for God to give us an undivided heart and then for us to allow that devotion to lapse and for us to become half-hearted in our following of Jesus. King David is famously described by God as 'a man after my own heart; he will do everything I want him to do' (1 Samuel 13:14; Acts 13:22). Yet even King David lost his focus on God, let his eyes wander and used his power to sleep with Bathsheba.[143] The Bible says he 'took' her (ESV), implying a fetching, seizing or even snatching. Not only did he abuse her but he then murdered her husband to cover up his selfish sin. This is an example of a wholehearted follower of God whose heart then divided into two completely different parts, intentions and behaviours. Being divided in our heart means that people become confused by us and hurt, used and vulnerable.

142. 1 Chronicles 28:9; 1 Kings 8:61; 2 Kings 20:3.
143. 2 Samuel 11:4.

We end up saying and doing things we do not want to do, and not doing the things we want to do. Paul says in Romans 7:21-25 how 'wretched' a way of living this is.

Fortunately, King David was convicted of this hardness of heart by a prophetic parable given by the prophet Nathan. Reason alone would not have got through the thick walls of David's selfish thinking. But the work of the Holy Spirit revealed the kind of injustice that he was allowing himself to be ruled by in his heart, and he confessed and repented. He experienced the forgiveness of God and wrote in Psalm 51:17, 'My sacrifice, O God, is a broken spirit; a broken and contrite heart you, God, will not despise.'

A divided heart resists the love of God. A broken heart can become a whole again.

Questions

When have you known that you have been double-hearted in some way? What did it do to you and others around you?

Why do our hearts so often resist reason? How does the Holy Spirit get through to hard-hearted people in the Bible to help them confess, repent and be released?

Who do you know who is wholehearted in their devotion to Jesus? What is it in their lives that you admire and what could you learn from them?

How do you best strengthen your heart and reorientate your heart towards Jesus? Is it in prayer, the Bible, fellowship, worship, solitude? Do you have a rhythm where you can do this intentionally to remain closely in step with the Holy Spirit?

> For the eyes of the Lord move to and fro throughout the earth that He may strongly support those whose heart is completely His' (1 Chron 16:9, NASB1995). Pray (for each other) to be seen by God and to be strengthened and supported in your hearts for the challenges and desires that you are facing.

Artist: Kathryn Timms

Most of my metal work is inspired by the Greek word *Katartizo* which means more than restoration and talks of being re-storied, fitted for perfect purpose. The fish being reformed from scrap and the box lights exploring being restored to light. My chairs are a recent piece I did for my MA in which I am exploring the impact of creativity in journeying with grief and the need for lament and acts of remembrance. The chairs are paper nets which hold rubbings of the chairs my mum would have sat in. They are designed as conversational pieces that invite us to consider the story and sit with the presence, absence and mixed emotions of loss and love of the grief journey. All have story at the centre of what I do.

(Kathryn Timms)

PART FIVE

On The Road

Loving and listening as we choose to follow Jesus wherever he goes

Classroom

What might happen on the road?

As an introduction to this final chapter, I thought I would share this story of what it means to follow Jesus. I have just heard it from a friend who, with her husband, runs a language school and leads a church community. They live in a place where it is not easy to be a follower of Jesus, so I have taken out the names.

> I would like to share with you the story of our friend, J, and the way we have seen God work in her life in a truly miraculous way over the last two months. For me, her life is an example of being desperately hungry for more of God.
>
> It was about 10 o'clock on a Saturday night, we had finished our usual church gathering, said goodbye to the last guests and just had that feeling of ok, it's the weekend, we can now relax, switch off. But then we hear the door opening in the church hall, we'd obviously forgotten to lock it, and then there is just this loud voice shouting P, P! I had no idea who this was, but it's quite normal for people just to walk into our house, so I went down to see. And it was J. J who we had prayed for all summer because we knew that she had fallen back into her old life of drink and drug dependency. J who we had prayed for because they had taken her into the psychiatric hospital because she was in such a bad way. J who we had prayed for just a month earlier when she was in intensive care and we didn't know whether or not she would make it through. J who we had prayed for to go to a Christian rehab centre and who had then gone there, but she had only lasted three days before getting herself a taxi and leaving.
>
> And here she is. J had somehow in her very unsober state got herself to our house, not because she was wanting to sort her life out with the Lord, but just because she had nowhere to go and sleep. As we stand in the doorway, she starts trying to explain how she is locked out of her flat,

she has lost her keys, and she has nowhere to go. Could she just stay one night with us? 'Well yes, of course, you better come in.'

So J comes in, has some food and a shower and we try to have a conversation. But the conversation is not going anywhere because the paranoid thoughts that come from the drugs are just so real for her that it's hard to have a conversation without her going back to her paranoia. 'OK,' we say, 'you need rest, but you need prayer.' J agrees to this. R was at home so we ask R to go downstairs to the hall and play worship while we are upstairs praying with J but with the worship in the background. And we pray. I pray. And we just realise we need Jesus 'cos none of us know what else to do.

After that, J slept. I decided to sleep in the room next to her so I could hear what was going on. I kept checking her as you do a newborn baby when they sleep, or if your child is sick. Are they OK, are they really still sleeping?

J not only slept through the night, she slept that day till 5 o'clock in the afternoon. Then she woke up, we read Psalms, prayed, she ate. A and I said she could stay for a week. And went back to sleep.

And that's what happened for the first three days. J would really just sleep and eat, pray, read the Bible and go back to sleep again.

We started reading a study book with her called *One Step at a Time*[144] which basically helps people with addictions to find freedom in Jesus. So, we did these lessons every day. And J just got it. And when she would read the Bible verses in the lessons, she would say, 'Oh that's about me. Oh, that's what I need!'

144. Danika K. Frank, *One Step at a Time: A Twelve Step Biblical Guide to Recovery* (Orlando, FL: Luminous Publishing, 2021).

It was amazing for me to see the Holy Spirit just working in her life. And all the time she was just wanting to pray and worship, because she realised that Jesus was her only answer. Jesus was her only way to be free from the drugs and the cigarettes and the alcohol. And the only way for a new life of meaning and purpose.

A and I would pray a lot for her because we have no experience of this sort of ministry. We didn't know what to do. We had heard about how hard it is for people to get free from addiction, especially on these synthetic drugs or salts as they call them which mess with the brain. So, we just kept praying and asking God to help her, to help us.

But it was so amazing because really apart from praying and walking with J on her journey, we didn't need to do anything. God just did it all and freed her from the dependency pretty much without any withdrawal symptoms. J was surrounded by the loving church family and different people would come and see her during the day so she wouldn't be on her own and we would pray together, read Psalms each morning, do the lesson in the afternoon and pray again in the evening.

And J just started living her life with Jesus. She would pray such prayers of desperation. And nearly every day she would say, P, I just need to worship, play 'our song'. Her song? 'This is the Air I Breathe'.[145] J sings this song nearly every day. I never really thought much of that song. But now I realise that I have probably never felt desperate for Jesus. I have Jesus in my life, but I have kind of got used to that. Of course, I know that I am lost for eternity without Jesus, but I don't experience the reality of the hopelessness of my life if it wasn't for Jesus.

145. www.youtube.com/watch?v=Rg9wV0nfvgg (accessed 4.11.25).

But J does. And every time she sings that she needs Jesus, she sings so loudly, so out of tune, but so from her heart. It's not so much a song as a cry of her heart because she needs Jesus, his presence and she really knows that, she really means it. She has experienced the lostness and desperation of living her life without him. And she is so desperate for now to be different. A new life. A different life with Jesus.

About a week after J had been living with us we had a day of prayer and worship. We sang another favourite song of J's, 'His name is Jesus'.[146] After we sang, I went to give J a hug. It was meant to just be a 'passing hug', but J just clung to me and wouldn't let go. She is weeping and weeping. And as she wept, I suddenly realise she is praying. First thanking the Lord for accepting her, thanking him for saving her, and then telling him how much she needs him. And as I hold her as she weeps and prays, I'm weeping too, because I realise the prodigal has truly come home. Not really expecting to have a restored life with Jesus, just coming because she had nowhere to sleep. Suddenly I have the privilege of being the one who stretches out the loving arms of welcome, and I am humbled to be part of God touching and restoring J to her place as his child in the family.

And as I hug her and she keeps weeping, I realise the prodigal also came home not expecting anything but maybe just to have something to eat. It was the welcome of the Father that restored the prodigal, although the prodigal had had to come. I am learning and seeing so much more of the transforming power of Jesus to bring freedom, I am humbled seeing J's passion and love for Jesus, her complete dependency on him.

146. www.youtube.com/watch?v=deiWQo1GZmE (accessed 4.11.25).

> To the Jews who had believed him, Jesus said, 'If you hold to my teaching, you are really my disciples. Then you will know the truth, and the truth will set you free.' They answered him, 'We are Abraham's descendants and have never been slaves of anyone. How can you say that we shall be set free?' Jesus replied, 'Very truly I tell you, everyone who sins is a slave to sin. Now a slave has no permanent place in the family, but a son belongs to it for ever. So if the Son sets you free, you will be free indeed.'
>
> (John 8:31-36)

> Everyone thinks we are helping J. But actually, she is the one helping us. When did I last say, 'Oh I just really need to worship. Oh, I really need Jesus. Thank you, Jesus that I'm alive. Thank you, Jesus for saving me'? Maybe that's what I need. Maybe God has sent to us to show us that we are the ones who need to be hungry for more of Jesus, because without him we really are nothing and we can do nothing.
>
> Jesus, I'm desperate for you, I'm so dependent on you, I'm lost without you, I am nothing and can do nothing without you. Thank you for the freedom from sin and the new life You have given both J and me.
>
> (P.R., Autumn 2025)

This is a story about ordinary people like you and me. They were ready to be interrupted. They were ready to love with all their heart, soul, mind and strength. They were out of their depth in the problems they were facing (but how wonderful that they were led by Jesus to a similar kind of extraordinary ministry that Jackie Pullinger has developed in Hong Kong[147]). All three dimensions of up, in and out are seen in this story –

147. /www.ststephenssociety.com/ (accessed 4.11.25).

and the result is fresh understanding, praise and freedom for everyone following Jesus together on the road.

On the road as Deuteronomy people

> Now what I am commanding you today is not too difficult for you or beyond your reach. It is not up in heaven, so that you have to ask, 'Who will ascend into heaven to get it and proclaim it to us so that we may obey it?' Nor is it beyond the sea, so that you have to ask, 'Who will cross the sea to get it and proclaim it to us so that we may obey it?' No, the word is very near you; it is in your mouth and in your heart so that you may obey it.
>
> See, I set before you today life and prosperity, death and destruction. For I command you today to love the LORD your God, to walk in obedience to him, and to keep his commands, decrees and laws; then you will live and increase, and the LORD your God will bless you in the land you are entering to possess.
>
> But if your heart turns away and you are not obedient, and if you are drawn away to bow down to other gods and worship them, I declare to you this day that you will certainly be destroyed. You will not live long in the land you are crossing the Jordan to enter and possess.
>
> This day I call the heavens and the earth as witnesses against you that I have set before you life and death, blessings and curses. Now choose life, so that you and your children may live and that you may love the LORD your God, listen to his voice, and hold fast to him. For the LORD is your life, and he will give you many years in the land he swore to give to your fathers, Abraham, Isaac and Jacob.
>
> (Deuteronomy 30:11-20)

We read in Part 1 about the theme of walking in the way of Yahweh that runs through the Hebrew Bible. The NIV Bible translates 'way' or 'road' as 'obedience' here in Deuteronomy – 'walking in obedience'. In these verses above there is a choice to make and consequences. The consequences are not necessarily rewards and punishments from a controlling God. Walking in obedience leads to experiencing eternal life now – even when there are challenges, disappointments and tragedies, God is with us and will shepherd us so that spiritually we continue to inherit his promises and eternal life. Turning away to follow other gods means that this spiritual life is stifled and hard to access. God still cares and loves, but ignoring his word and living selfishly is simply not how humans were designed to be. This leads to toil, sweat, pain and death. So these commands of Moses are not threats but compassionate warnings about how to live. Follow the way of Yahweh – and in the New Covenant follow the way of Jesus – and this is how we best navigate life, for ourselves and also for the world around us.

> I'm reminded that formation isn't about performance but about becoming, it's a journey. True discipleship calls us to take responsibility and to step up and follow Jesus – to embrace our God-given identity, to face our fears, and have the courage to walk with humility, strength, and resilience in a broken world. Spiritual formation helps sharpen our character, strengthens our choices, and enables us to reflect the Jesus we follow with authenticity – not just on the mountaintop but in the mundane, the messy, and the mission field of everyday life.
>
> (Warren Evans, Sports Chaplaincy UK)

At the end of all Moses' teaching, he says to Israel that there is a choice to make. He uses strong words here in chapter 30 – blessing and cursing; life and death – and urges them to 'choose life'. Soon Moses will die and Israel will be without their teacher and architect. Joshua will take over, but as the one who leads them into the promised land, not as a shepherd in the same way that Moses had been. Moses was the miracle worker, the one through whom God set them free from Egypt; who healed them, provided manna from heaven and water from the rock. The question for Israel now is how will they continue with a life of following God, into the promised land and beyond? What does it look like to encounter God and hear his voice and then put it into practice, day by day and generation by generation? The people who met Jesus in Mark's Gospel faced a similar challenge. Now that I am free and healed, how do I follow Jesus on the road?

The essence of this new journey into the promised land is not about external words and teaching like it was in the wilderness. It is about hearts that are changed. This is written in such a way in this chapter, 30:1-10, that we can see how changed hearts are central. The structure is chiastic which, without the help of bold, italics, large fonts, page layout, is one of the most common ways that the Hebrew Bible is written to underline a central point.[148] Each phrase goes in towards and comes out from the central point – that God will circumcise our hearts and our children's hearts (D). And around this central point we see these circles: We take God's word to heart as we turn/return to him (A). We walk in obedience (B). Our lives prosper and God delights in us (C). Notice too, at the start, middle and end, the phrase: 'with all your heart and with all your soul'.

148. See Wright, *New International Bible Commentary: Deuteronomy.*

When all these blessings and curses I have set before you come on you and you take them to *heart* wherever the Lord your God disperses you among the nations,

A) and when you and your children *return* to the LORD your God . . . (v. 2)

B) and obey him *with all your heart and with all your soul* . . . (v. 2)

C) . . . He will make you more *prosperous* and numerous than your *ancestors.* (vv. 3-5)

D) *The LORD your God will circumcise your hearts and the hearts of your descendants, so that you may love him with all your heart and with all your soul, and live.* (v. 6)

C) . . . The LORD will again *delight* in you and make you *prosperous,* just as he *delighted* in your *ancestors* . . . (v. 9)

B) . . . if you *obey* the LORD your God and keep his commands and decrees . . . v. 10

A) . . . *turn* to the LORD your God *with all your heart and with all your soul.* v. 10

(my emphases)

I am grateful for the apps that have made daily practices more accessible to all. I enjoy the Lectio daily readings and reflections but also the Bible in one-year readings that can also be listened to. I also make the moments count – time in the car, boiling the kettle or walking can be used for prayer. It is good to pray before and after sending emails, and social media updates from organisations, charities and individuals are fantastic prompts to pray. Rather than scrolling past, I often linger and pray for the ministry or the issue being raised.

(Cathy Madavan, Speaker and Author)

Heart and soul is not necessarily something that comes easily to us the older we become. Age brings with it cynicism, tiredness and a certain grumpiness of spirit. Moses seemed to get grumpier as he got older. Yet being an obedient follower is clearly not a dry and ruled based expectation. It is about exuberance, effort, fellowship and praise. I notice in Moses' teaching that he counteracts this resistance to heart and soul in two ways.

He always refers to children, and he starts to sing.

Loving wholeheartedly is childlike. It is about abandonment and trust. It is passionate and carefree. Jesus said that the kingdom of God belongs to children. If we cannot receive it like a child then we cannot enter it.[149] How interesting that the kingdom of God – which is all that is described by Moses – has to be received! Not earned, or bought, or won in a competition or exam but received – which means it has been freely given. Children are great at receiving. They are quite able to snatch the gift out of your kindly proffered hand before there's a chance for the niceties of how generous you have been and how thankful they should be. That is not to defend ungrateful brat-like behaviour – but a child's heart may not yet have had the knocks, disappointments and hurts that then throw up a wall of mistrust, fear and suspicion. Children seem more able than adults to play with abandon, to sing, to move freely and to generally break polite rules when they are excited and pleased about something. This is the attitude that Moses is calling out from the people of Israel. So he insists that they spend time teaching these things with their families around them, eating with their children and generally spending

149. Matthew 18:3.

time with their children, for the sake of their children's future. Being with the children for the sake of the children changes the dynamic from resentful, hard-hearted adulting, to fun, unordered, hopeful childlikeness. In fact, Joshua and Caleb were the oldest Israelites at this time but in Joshua 14, Caleb behaves like a teenager (in a good way!):

> So here I am today, eighty-five years old! I am still as strong today as the day Moses sent me out; I'm just as vigorous to go out to battle now as I was then. Now give me this hill country that the LORD promised me that day. You yourself heard then that the Anakites were there and their cities were large and fortified, but, the LORD helping me, I will drive them out just as he said.
>
> (Joshua 14:10-12)

We have produced several books and resources too including; *Serve* (the core mission of the body of Christ; *Way Maker* by Josh Green and Debra Green;[150] *Mountain-Moving Prayer* by Debra Green and Dave Roberts;[151] *ROC Your World* by Debra Green.[152] Also resources like *101 Community Ideas*[153] and a new community development course with the Nazarene Theological College.[154]

I highly recommend Cris Rogers' book *Making Disciples* and the website; https://wearemakingdisciples.com

(Debra Green, Redeeming Our Communities)

150. Published: Manchester: Redeeming Our Communities, 2025.
151. London: SPCK, 2019.
152. Kent: River Publishing & Media Ltd, 2014.
153. Download for free at https://roc.uk.com/wp-content/uploads/2018/09/101CommunityIdeas2.pdf (accessed 17.11.25).
154. https://roc.uk.com/roc-community-development-award/ (accessed 17.11.25).

This is heart and soul talk! And it's coming from a seasoned follower of eighty-five years old! Jesus encouraged older men like Nicodemus to be born again – and implied in this the need for him to overcome his closed mind to see the kingdom of God, in John 3. We see Nicodemus emerging with tentative boldness among his peers by defending Jesus in John 7, and then, with another fearful older adult, Joseph, giving their heart and soul to Jesus by approaching Pilate, and burying Jesus with huge amounts of 'myrrh and aloes' (John 19:38-39).

Heart and soul is vigour, generosity, boldness and childlike abandon.

Heart and soul is also song. Years before Aretha Franklin and Ray Charles, Moses was a soul singer. The last thing he does, after all this teaching and before he dies, is to sing two songs.

> One of the books that has impacted my spiritual life the most is, *A Resilient Life* (Gordon MacDonald)[155] who in his later years wrote about all the questions you ask of life and faith in the various decades of your life. It is an incredible book as he also lays out ways in which we can run the discipleship race well so that we are more fruitful towards the end of the race rather than at the beginning.
>
> One of the other disciplines of my life is to regularly ensure I put myself in a context that is not like the one I live, usually in the developing world where I sense and experience poverty but invariably sense and experience faith at a different level.
>
> (Leon Evans, Lifecentral Church, Further Faster Network)

155. Published: Nashville, TN: Thomas Nelson, 2006.

The first song in chapter 32 sums up the covenant and Moses' teaching.

> Listen, you heavens, and I will speak;
> hear, you earth, the words of my mouth.
> Let my teaching fall like rain
> and my words descend like dew,
> like showers on new grass,
> like abundant rain on tender plants.
>
> (Deuteronomy 32:1-2)

Like any good soul song, it is all about love and loss. God as a rock, a parent, the maker, who is constantly rejected and let down by unfaithful Israel – and yet keeps loving and giving of himself. When we are called to love God with all our heart and soul, we are called into the kind of love he has for us. This is sacrificial, generous, patient and kind. Loving with all our heart and soul is a reflection of the love of God for humanity, which has abandoned him and gone their own way. But God the lover, in Jesus, lays down his life for his loved one in the hope that they will respond and return. Paul sums up the God of Moses' song in Romans 8:31-32: 'If God is for us, who can be against us? He who did not spare his own Son, but gave him up for us all – how will he not also, along with him, graciously give us all things?'

The second song in chapter 33 is a song of blessing over each of the tribes of Israel.

The way of Yahweh is the way of blessing and prophesying, speaking out righteousness and justice. The Apostle Paul describes prophecy as 'for their strengthening, encouraging and comfort . . . try to excel in those that build up the church' (1 Corinthians 14:3,12). The last thing Moses does is to bless his people, to strengthen them and let them know how God sees them. Simeon and Anna, also as older people, did this for Jesus and his family in the temple when they saw him as a baby in Luke 2:25-38. Jesus, in his final moments on the cross, declared forgiveness for his murderers in Luke 23:34, the promise of paradise for the thief in Luke 23:43, and family for his mother and friends in John 19:26-27. This approach is a theme picked up by Paul who urges the church at Galatia to walk by the Spirit, not biting and devouring one another, but loving our neighbour as ourselves. He says that being in step with the Spirit means that we will carry one another's burdens on the way: 'Therefore, as we have opportunity, let us do good to all people, especially to those who belong to the family of believers' (Galatians 5:14 – 6:10).

So we see Moses putting what he teaches into practice, by sharing the love of God and encouraging the people to live well and to walk out their lives both in heaven and on the earth. The final line of his song reflects his final action. He sings 'you will tread on their heights' (Deuteronomy 33:29) and with that, he himself walks up the mountain one final time before he dies.

> Then Moses climbed Mount Nebo from the plains of Moab to the top of Pisgah, opposite Jericho. There the Lord showed him the whole land – from Gilead to Dan, all of Naphtali, the territory of Ephraim and Manasseh, all the land of Judah as far as the Mediterranean Sea, the Negev and the whole region from the Valley of Jericho, the City of Palms, as far as Zoar. Then the Lord said to him, 'This is the land I promised on oath to Abraham, Isaac and Jacob when I said, "I will give it to your descendants." I have let you see it with your eyes, but you will not cross over into it.'

Enoch is famous for walking with God, and then the Bible says 'he was no more' (Genesis 5:24)! Noah, Abraham and Isaac are all described as walking with God. This final journey of Moses up the mountain is one more chance to see him walk with his friend and survey the promised land. This steady rhythm of trust and openness – through the valleys and also up in the mountain heights – is the call of a disciple. The New Testament writer John calls it 'walking in the truth' and describes it beautifully in 2 John 1:4 – 6:4:

> It has given me great joy to find some of your children walking in the truth, just as the Father commanded us. And now, dear lady, I am not writing you a new command but one we have had from the beginning. I ask that we love one another. And this is love: that we walk in obedience to his commands. As you have heard from the beginning, his command is that you walk in love.

I remember hearing – being a Christian without reading the Bible and praying is like living without breathing. We did a Confident Disciples series (which is on our website)[156] – teaching at the front, discussion in small groups but then activities/actions to put things into practice. Being a confident disciple is not just about more knowledge which we should want and grow in but the exercise of taking what we have learned on a Sunday into the world. Remembering, the win isn't the outcome, the win is being willing and trying for Jesus.

(Nicky Wong, All Hallows Church, Bow)

156. www.allhallowsbow.org.uk (accessed 17.11.25).

On the road with Jesus in Mark's Gospel

> Then he called the crowd to him along with his disciples and said: 'Whoever wants to be my disciple must deny themselves and take up their cross and follow me. For whoever wants to save their life will lose it, but whoever loses their life for me and for the gospel will save it.
>
> (Mark 8:34-35)

Apart from going to church and being part of a small group, I use a daily devotional – my favourites are *Streams in the Desert*[157] and *The Bible with Nicky and Pippa Gumbel*[158] – I mix it up from time to time. In terms of wider reading, I regularly revisit Roy Hession's *The Calvary Road*,[159] and AW Tozer's *The Knowledge of the Holy*,[160] and I've really appreciated newer injections including *Praying Like Monks, Living Like Fools*, by Tyler Staton,[161] and John Mark Comer's *The Ruthless Elimination of Hurry*.[162]

My husband and I pray together daily. We have a weekly sabbath to make space and time to be, to pray, to learn from others, and enjoy God's wonderful creation in the great outdoors with our little dog. We also value Christian conferences – there's something about arriving with the expectation we will hear God's voice more clearly when we make time and space like this – and we usually do!

Beyond some of these things, I invite outside accountability from Christians, and I set aside four days a year for spiritual direction and reflection.

(Alexandra Huggins, Faith in Later Life)

157. Published: Grand Rapids, MI: Zondervan, 1997.
158. https://bible.alpha.org/en/ (accessed 4.11.25).
159. Published by Christian Literature Crusade, 1964.
160. Published: San Antonio, TX: Bibliotech Press, 2016.
161. Published: London: Hodder & Stoughton, 2022.
162. Published: London: Hodder & Stoughton, 2019.

This is another way of saying 'Love God with all your heart, soul, mind and strength' but here Jesus uses the language of following to describe what it means to be a disciple. This is a strong theme in Mark's Gospel. 'Come with me', 'Follow me', and 'they followed him' are mentioned many times in the book as well as instructions to his disciples to go somewhere.[163]

Jesus models a life that is committed to being on the road. He sees life lived in the Spirit as one of movement and purpose. It is not about learning some subjects and sitting an exam. Instead, it is a journey, and loving God wholeheartedly is tested on that journey and refined by circumstances, people and events. There is a phrase that Mark uses often, especially in the middle of his Gospel, *'On the way'*. (This Greek word *hodos* also means road or journey). Each time Jesus predicts his death it is as he is 'on the way' – which makes his view of

> For me the heart of being a disciple is to respond daily to the invitation of Jesus 'follow me.' This is an invitation to not only follow the teachings of Jesus (our Rabbi) but to go where he goes, to do what he does, to think like he thinks, to respond like he would respond. Religion says 'change then follow' but Jesus says 'follow then change!' It's in our daily commitment to follow him that we will become more like him. To me discipleship is not about how much I know it's about how much I put into practice of what I know. It's a journey of becoming not just doing, it's also a journey of discovery, of myself, of the world and of who God is.
>
> (Leon Evans, Lifecentral Church, Further Faster Network)

163. Mark 1:17,18; 2:15; 6:31; 10:21.

his crucifixion intentional and very much part of his mission.[164] These are the words used when Jesus is about to set out 'on the journey' when he meets the rich young ruler who ends up deciding not to follow him, and then of Bartimaeus who is sitting 'by the roadside' and then after being healed of blindness, follows Jesus 'along the road'. (Mark 10:17,46-52). This phrase also opens Mark's Gospel within the three references from the Hebrew Bible in Exodus, Isaiah and Malachi. The role of the messenger, whether we read that as an angel, or John the Baptist and even Jesus sent by the Father – and certainly our own role – is to prepare 'the way' for others (Mark 1:1-3).

Living sent

We have already seen that the apostles are the 'sent ones' and that 'God sent his . . . only son' (1 John 4:9). Being sent by Jesus is still part of being a follower. We are on the road but may be sent ahead. The disciples were sent on ahead to Bethsaida while Jesus 'dismissed the crowd' (Mark 6:45), and he 'sent [them] ahead' to Samaria, and on mission in pairs (Luke 9:52;

> I have found the P.R.A.Y. method (Pete Greig/ 24-7 Prayer) a really helpful tool to help me connect with God, not just in prayer but in everyday life. Pause-Rejoice-Ask-Yield. Reminding myself of who God is, how great he is and how much he loves me and has given me hope and new life, that my life is best lived in a response of love to him and love to those around me and that every part of who I am and what I do is important.
>
> (Peter Wilson, Spring Harvest, Physiotherapist)

164. Mark 8:27; 9:33; 10:32

10:1). He also sent them ahead to find the colt tied up ready for his entry into Jerusalem in Mark 11:2. In fact, being sent is an integral part of being a follower. It is a way of life. I know a church whose slogan for themselves is Live Sent.[165] It is how they want to live life, as sent ones wherever that may be. Being sent as a disciple also means being sent back home, to work out our discipleship among our family, friends and neighbours. Jesus appreciates how this is the place to ground our lives; to be worshipful, connect with others and practise being on mission. The man who is lowered down through the roof into Jesus' house has four great friends who are determined, supportive, courageous and full of faith. The man obviously already understands something of fellowship, but Jesus deals with his need for forgiveness as well as healing his body. And then Jesus sends him home. Jesus trusts him with carrying the gospel within his body and among his own people.[166] The same happens with the man called Legion, who is set free and healed by Jesus. This man obviously wants to join Jesus and follow him. But Jesus tells him to go home to his own people and witness there. The man will have been without family and friends for a long time and probably needs normality and security. But his total transformation meant that those who knew him would be amazed at the power of Jesus to change a life.[167]

Following Jesus, but not being a famous and important named apostle

In each of our Playground sections we have looked at stories in Mark's Gospel that compare those who do a good job of following Jesus with those who are not so good. In Mark's Gospel it is the named disciples and the devout religious

165. Shades Mountain Baptist Church, Birmingham, Alabama.
166. Mark 2:11-12.
167. Mark 5:15-20.

people who make a mess of things, or miss the point, or lose their excitement. It is the outsiders – that is the people who are unwell, the Gentiles, the sinners, and the women (mostly not even named) – who are usually those who begin to live a wholehearted life of devotion, upward to God but also inward to their friends and outward to their neighbours. Following is not so much about being publicly called and honoured by Jesus as it is about trusting that Jesus knows us and loves us and is worthy of our whole-life commitment. To deny ourselves, take up our cross and follow Jesus is how Jesus defines a disciple,[168] rather than having a name, a website, a podcast and numerous speaking gigs at all the main Christian events. Therefore, it is worth taking a look at those who are anonymous, treated as less special by those around, and even nervous about whether Jesus will want them, in order to see some good examples of what being a true follower looks like.

> Christian books have been like mentors I can return to again and again. John Ortberg's books were particularly helpful a few years ago, and authors writing about prayer, suffering, faith or biblical insight have been extremely helpful. Conferences and events have helpfully enlarged my faith and my thinking, although the context of our local church where the worship and teaching lived out in community is the crucible for discipleship. Crucially, however, I would say that seasoned leaders and disciples who have been mentors, friends and guides over the years have been absolutely essential. Without their support, challenge, insight and wisdom, I would have floundered many times. Good discipleship needs wise or experienced disciples coming alongside other disciples.
>
> (Cathy Madavan, Speaker and Author)

168. See Luke 9:23.

Women followers on the road with Jesus

Mark's Gospel ends formally at chapter 16:8 (most scholars agree that the final verses after this are a summing up of the disciples' mission after the resurrection, that were added to the Gospel.) Verse 8 is an abrupt end. There are women at the tomb – the disciples have fled of course, even before Jesus died – and a 'young man dressed in a white robe' (v. 15; 'an angel' according to Matthew 28:2-6) tells the women to go and tell Peter and the disciples that Jesus has risen and gone ahead of them to Galilee. (Note Mark's theme again of 'going ahead' and everyone having to follow!) The final line then is: 'Trembling and bewildered, the women went out and fled from the tomb. They said nothing to anyone, because they were afraid.'

This seems an odd and anticlimactic end! (Which is why some early Christians understandably and helpfully added the rest of the chapter!) On first reading it looks like they fearfully run away just like the male disciples, abandoning the mission of Jesus. But we know from the other Gospels that they went and told Peter and the disciples straight away. This means then that they actually obeyed the angel to the letter, as reverent and awestruck disciples. The Apostle Paul uses the same language as is used here of the women – in 'fear and trembling' – to describe wholehearted discipleship, adding words like obedience, crucifixion and sincerity of heart to characterise this attitude in 1 Corinthians 2:3; 2 Corinthians 7:15; Ephesians 6:5 and Philippians 2:12. Scholars such as Jeff Aernie, Larry Hurtado and Susan Miller all agree that the women in Mark's Gospel are the examples of discipleship that should be followed, albeit recognising that Mark presents Jesus as the most perfect example for us of the obedient wholehearted lover of God and his neighbour.[169]

169. Larry W. Hurtado, eds Zuleika Rodgers, Margaret Daly-Denton and Anne Fitzpatrick McKinley, 'The Women, the Tomb, and the Climax of Mark' in *A Wandering Galilean: Essays in Honour of Seàn Freyne*, (Leiden: Brill, 2009), pp. 427-450.
Jeffrey W. Aernie, *Narrative Discipleship: Portraits of Women in the Gospel of Mark* (Eugene, OR: Wipf and Stock Publishers, 2018), p. 120.
Susan Miller, Women in Mark's Gospel (Edinburgh: T&T Clark, 2004).

Jeff Aernie defines Mark's ideal of discipleship – demonstrated by the narratives of eight of the women described – as 'restored life', 'kingdom speech', 'sacrificial action' and 'cruciformity'. Examples that Mark gives us include the Syrophoenician woman, the woman with the issue of blood and the poor widow. Jesus' conversation with the Syrophoenician woman in Mark 7:24-30 is an odd one. It looks like Jesus is being critical and offensive towards her as a Gentile, even though he does eventually cast out the demon from her daughter. Jesus has deliberately gone to Tyre, a place with a history of being Israel's enemy, now Greek in culture; and Mark emphasises that the woman is a Gentile and from Syrophoenicia – letting us know she really is an outsider! As soon as she hears Jesus is there she comes to him, and not only that, falls at his feet, and not only that, calls him Lord – the only person to call him this in the Gospel. And then she keeps on asking him to cast out a demon from her daughter. She is determined, forceful, humble, faith-filled and believes in his lordship. A remarkable person! Jesus says, 'First let the children eat all they want, . . . for it is not right to take the children's bread and toss it to the dogs' (Mark 7:27). That sounds rude to me. So why is he suddenly talking about food, children and dogs? Matthew's version of the story in Matthew 15 emphasises Matthew's own Gospel theme that Jesus was sent first to the 'lost sheep of Israel'. (He also adds, that true to their usual form, the disciples were fed up with her!) Here, Jesus is saying that his priority so far has been to feed the children – of Israel. And he has just done that by

> My journey of discipleship is about learning to trust the Lord in every situation and standing firm on the promises of the Lord.
>
> (Rosie Giles, Spring Harvest)

feeding the 5,000 so much bread and fish that there's enough left over for the whole nation – symbolised by the twelve baskets! He has then been criticised by the religious people for letting his disciples eat without ritual washing, so he declares that food is clean for all. Then suddenly he comes here to Tyre, a Gentile culture. It has also been noted that the word used for dogs here is actually doggies – little dogs, puppies or even lapdogs. So Jesus is describing, in parable story form – hence the imagery of children and doggies – his mission so far. It has been to the children, many of whom have eaten their fill and some whom have just been resentful, but now he is extending himself out further to the Gentiles.

The woman responds with boldness, and grasps Jesus' style, returning brilliantly his clever imagery. She joins in with the parable style, adding details of the food table so that it now appears to be inside a home (which is important to Mark, remember). Here, the bread, now in crumbs which are small like the children and doggies, feeds the doggies under the table. She uses a different word for children. Rather than the word Jesus uses, *teknon*, which highlights offspring – and in his parable, the nation of Israel – she uses the word *paidon*. This is the word used for specific children: Jesus as an infant,

> For me spiritual formation is how behaviours and attitudes have become 'instinctive' over time. Knowing how Jesus loves me and calls me to live, and being *empowered by the Holy Spirit* to really know this on the best and worst of days, gives me a steadiness and a strength that's hard to explain without God, and which I hope speaks a message of what's possible with God.
>
> (Alexandra Huggins, Faith in Later Life)

the children who Jesus heals and blesses, and those that are part of the crowds listening to and following Jesus. She is highlighting children who may learn and join in with him. And she truly believes that she and her daughter can belong in the house and join in with the feast. Jesus tells her that her daughter is delivered – because of her answer! He has not even had to travel there, touch, speak or spit. He tells her to go, just like he tells so many of the other healed people who have now become wholehearted disciples. And then Jesus leaves Tyre. That was it! Just like going through Samaria and meeting the woman at the well, or crossing the sea to set free Legion. She and her daughter appeared to be the reason for his mission to that place, and from that point he fully embraces more Gentile territory. He heals a deaf man who finds it hard to talk. Then he feeds the 4,000 – which is a repeat of the earlier feeding story but this time demonstrating that all the nations can be fed and become satisfied, with seven baskets left over, symbolically now referring to the Gentiles. Meeting the Syrophoenician woman may not have changed Jesus' mind as some commentators say, but certainly this encounter was the turning point for broadening out his ministry. She is clever and faith-filled. She is a reminder of the woman at the well, who seems to me to be the brightest person Jesus meets, with the best and most fulfilling conversation he has. The woman of

> I try to bring Jesus into every part of life – not just my 'spiritual' moments. Whether I'm helping someone with their health journey, encouraging a friend, serving in church, leading the PTFA or making everyday choices that reflect kingdom values, I'm learning to invite him in.
>
> (Gaynor van der Burton, FitFish)

Tyre is a great example of one who comes to Jesus worshipfully and is sent by Jesus obediently.

Fear and trembling boldness is also seen in the woman who has been bleeding for twelve years in Mark 5:25-34. She has heard about Jesus so she comes up and touches his cloak 'because she thought, "If I just touch his clothes, I will be healed."' That is faith! Like the Syrophoenician, she hears, travels, and then falls at Jesus' feet. 'You see the people crowding against you,' his disciples answered, 'and yet you can ask, "Who touched me?"' 'Jesus realised that power has gone out from him', and she knew 'what had happened to her'. Already there is an invisible relationship of deep knowing between them both – a stronger bond than is experienced by the sarcastic disciples at that point! 'Trembling with fear, [she] told him the whole truth.' Of course she is worried that she has overstepped the mark of decorum, and everyone is watching her, especially these resentful disciples. She tells the whole truth – confessing it all but also allowing the whole story of her life to come pouring out. This is not just being scared of Jesus, it is trembling with excitement and wonder. It is giving our testimony through tears and laughter, our gratitude and praise meaning we can't stop talking. Jesus calls her 'Daughter' – she is not just a follower but one who belongs to the Father and the community of Israel. He sends her on her way, in peace and freedom from suffering. What

> My desire is to encourage, excite, and enthuse others to empower and enable them to excel . . . to be the best they can be for the Lord.
>
> (Rosie Giles, Spring Harvest)

a beautiful relationship between a daughter of God and the Saviour Jesus!

Finally, the scene where Jesus watches a poor widow giving all she has to the temple treasury is an example of a devoted heart. Jesus and the woman do not interact so there is no indication that she ends up following him as a disciple. Nevertheless, Jesus calls his disciples to himself in order to use her as an example for his teaching.

> Many rich people threw in large amounts. But a poor widow came and put in two very small copper coins, worth only a few cents.
>
> (Mark 12:41-44)

Mark uses masculine vocabulary to describe the rich people, but the widow is female, widowed and poor. This is a stark contrast between powerful and well-resourced people and someone who is at the very extreme edge of society and her ability to survive. Earlier in chapter 10 Jesus has encountered

> The most transformative practice for me has been finding someone who is already following Jesus and learning from them. At eighteen, I realised I needed a mentor, someone further along in their walk with Christ who could encourage and challenge me. Over the years, mentorship has taken many forms, but it remains the practice I recommend to everyone. True discipleship is not simply about meeting for coffee once a week; it is about sitting at someone's feet, watching how they live with Jesus, and growing alongside them.
>
> (Sammy Jabangwe Hanton, The Message Trust)

a man who is fulfilling all the commands that a disciple should obey. But he does not follow Jesus because he cannot give up his money. Jesus says, 'They all gave out of their wealth; but she, out of her poverty, put in everything – all she had to live on.' Jesus literally says that she has given her whole life (Greek: *bios*), meaning everything she relies upon. Therefore, he says: 'Truly I tell you, this poor widow has put more into the treasury than all the others.' This action is like the woman who anoints Jesus' head at Bethany in chapter 14. Both give way more than is expected. The woman at Bethany is criticised for wasting the money rather than giving it to the poor. Some commentators think similarly that this widow should not have given her money to the temple because Jesus criticises it in the scenes before and after. However, he does not appear to comment on whether her gift was a wise one or not – instead he highlights her as he does the woman at Bethany, and says how generous she has been. We can get caught up in the rights and wrongs of what to give to, what church to be part of, whether or not to align ourselves with certain ministries or people, that we then miss the point of being sacrificial and generous. A disciple is not one who critiques everything before committing, however clever this looks. A disciple is like a poor widow, whose Spirit-filled heart guides her head; like an ill woman who throws herself at Jesus' feet; and like a Gentile mother who humbly asks for food and deliverance from the Lord.

On the road: Next steps in Mark's Gospel

Even though the general agreement is that the Gospel that Mark wrote ends on that dramatic cliffhanger of chapter 16:8, the rest of the chapter has been included in most of the manuscripts of the Gospel, and from as early as the second century. So, even if it was not written by Mark himself, it has been accepted by the Church as a valid and important coda to his account. So it makes sense to use this ancient text as a summing up of how to take our next steps as disciples after meeting the resurrected Christ. We read in Mark 16:9-19:

> When Jesus rose early on the first day of the week, he appeared first to Mary Magdalene, out of whom he had driven seven demons. She went and told those who had been with him and who were mourning and weeping. When they heard that Jesus was alive and that she had seen him, they did not believe it.
>
> Afterwards Jesus appeared in a different form to two of them while they were walking in the country. These returned and reported it to the rest; but they did not believe them either.
>
> Later Jesus appeared to the Eleven as they were eating; he rebuked them for their lack of faith and their stubborn refusal to believe those who had seen him after he had risen.
>
> He said to them, 'Go into all the world and preach the gospel to all creation. Whoever believes and is baptised will be saved, but whoever does not believe will be condemned. And these signs will accompany those who believe: in my name they will drive out demons; they will speak in new tongues; they will pick up snakes with their hands; and when they drink deadly poison, it will not hurt them at all; they will place their hands on people who are ill, and they will get well.'
>
> After the Lord Jesus had spoken to them, he was taken up into heaven and he sat at the right hand of God.

Living Room

The disciples saw Jesus transfigured on the mountain, and heard God saying, 'Listen to Jesus.' Israel saw Moses come down the mountain, accompanied with fire and smoke, carrying the Word of God and instructions for how to live well. There is always a challenge for us, when we have met with God face to face, of how to put such an encounter into practice and not lose the wonder, momentum and conviction of these holy moments. It is often the case that when we have been at church, or at a Christian worship festival, or on a defined Christian mission, that we are fired up by great teaching, faith-filled companions, a room of thousands all worshipping. We then so desire to live differently and to imitate Jesus in every way. This desire is a true desire. It is not just fabricated or whipped up by an atmosphere of enthusiasm. When we are hearing God's Word, enjoying his presence, and purposefully sharing our faith, then of course our spirits are open and keen, hungry to be filled with the righteousness of God. Like the disciples of Jesus and Moses, our challenge is to then live this out when we come down the mountain; when we are no longer in the house surrounded by the exuberant faith of others; when the sending out does not have shouts of hallelujah and roads strewn with palm branches.

Walking together

Both Moses and Jesus are identified as people on a journey; in the wilderness with a huge bunch of followers who moan, rejoice, dance and rebel; and around Galilee and Jerusalem with large crowds who are amazed, twelve disciples who don't get it, and a random collection of people who throw in their lot 100 per cent. However, when we see Jesus walking together with the two disciples on the road to Emmaus in Luke 24:13-35 – them pouring out their hearts to this graciously listening stranger, and him opening their eyes to the truth of God's Scripture – we see what walking honestly together with Jesus really looks like. It ends in a home, around a meal table, and then a revelation of who Jesus is that so energises them they run to Jerusalem to declare the good news.

The book of Joshua, which follows Deuteronomy, is all about Joshua taking Israel on a new kind of journey, also. Not only do he and the people experience more of God's heart and mind, but they also discover new places of freedom; ways of living where they can put into practice the teaching of Moses they have just heard. This book has been compared to the book of Ephesians in the New Testament. Both are accounts about moving up into the high places, about identity and purpose, about how to sit, stand and walk in the presence of God while on the earth. Paul uses the word for walking around – *peripateo* – to describe a life of surrender, discovery, Christlike behaviour and submission to the power of the Holy Spirit. It is a walk of love, that we have to take together:

> Follow God's example, therefore, as dearly loved children and *walk in the way of love,* just as Christ loved us and gave himself up for us as a fragrant offering and sacrifice to God.
>
> (Ephesians 5:1-2)[170]

I love to walk, and, in the walking, I create space to be with God. I speak to him, I seek to listen to him, I see him in the creation around me. I look ahead and I look up!

As I take steps of faith, as I step out of my comfort zone and choose to rely on God (there is only God that I can truly rely on), I experience more of what it means to be a child of God.

(Damian Wharton, Scripture Union Northern Ireland)

170. NIV, my emphasis; See also 2:2; 2:10; 4:17; 5:2; 5:8; 5:15.

Stages on the journey

Chris Hodges, who is the founding pastor of Church of the Highlands in Birmingham, Alabama has written a book called *What's Next?: The Journey to Know God, Find Freedom, Discover Purpose, & Make a Difference.*[171] The YouVersion Bible app now has a twelve-day reading plan based on this book and there are plenty of churches who have taken this framework to help them in their process of making disciples. It outlines an idea of how to help people on their journey of

> I love church! Sundays are my best day. Corporate worship, rich teaching, seeing friends, it truly is the highlight of my week. In my early years of faith, I tried to maintain that same level of enthusiasm when Monday morning came and I very quickly realised that was impossible. I mean, does anyone have any enthusiasm for Mondays? I've learned that my love for Jesus is not tethered to my love for the church, and that lesson helped me grow in my everyday discipleship. It helped me grow in my faith because I wasn't reliant on others to teach me the Word or create a spiritual atmosphere. I had to embed discipline and rhythms into my everyday life to remain an enthusiastic disciple of Christ. For me, reflecting on what does it mean to be a disciple in our everyday life, it means to accept every day won't be our best, but our love for Jesus should be steadfast. It means taking ownership of our growth, so when Sunday does roll round, I'm not relying on it to fill me up for the week ahead, but I am there to worship and learn from a place of overflow.
>
> (Marie Aitken, Hillsong UK)

171. Published: Nashville, TN: HarperChristian Resources, 2019.

following Jesus. It is easy to see the progression of steps from finding out about who God is and knowing Jesus personally, then experiencing the freedom that the Holy Spirit brings us as our minds are changed and hearts set free, especially through practice and prayer. From there is the emphasis on gifts and calling, on the life that is modelled on the dimensions of up, in and out. Finally, there is the emphasis on actually living – behaving, acting and interacting in such a way that we bring the fragrance of Jesus and the impact of the kingdom of God to our world. It is a really helpful pattern for us to bear in mind. This journey, of course, never ends. We are always knowing God more deeply, finding more freedom, moving purposefully in new directions, and making a difference in all kinds of ways. The way of the kingdom of heaven is a never-ending exploration and experience of the heart of God. It is as we are on this road that we are formed by Christ.

> Most of my family, friends and neighbours don't know Jesus – living for him means making time for them, praying for them, supporting them to be all that God made them to be, weaving my story of God into conversations, and occasionally drawing a hard line, e.g. when I was recently invited to do recreational drugs with them. Of course, I said 'no'! It's about being loving, generous and carrying God's peace into the situations I'm invited into. In terms of my work, I have the incredible privilege of getting out of bed every day, to help people know Jesus – it's the dream job! Understanding the importance of this keeps me focused and energised around what matters; and so the day begins with prayer, I let go of situations that disappoint and do what I can to keep in step with Jesus.
>
> (Alexandra Huggins, Faith in Later Life)

Formation of the disciple

The apostle Paul's ambition for the church at Galatia (and for all of us) is that 'Christ is formed in you' (Galatians 4:19.) There has been an emphasis all through Church history on spiritual formation. This is how we build a life that can contain the Word and Spirit of God, and become a beautiful and powerful imitation of how Jesus lived on the earth. Robert Mulholland writes that when we see discipleship and spiritual formation as a process then we see that actually everything in life is about spiritual formation. It may be deeply personal but spiritual formation is the way of becoming more like Christ for the benefit of other people. 'And *whatever you do*, whether in word or deed, *do it all in the name of the Lord Jesus*, giving thanks to God the Father through him' (Colossians 3:17, my emphasis). If all of life is spiritual as well as physical then it is not a matter of whether we engage in spiritual formation or not – clearly we are being formed spiritually whoever we are and whatever we do. The question is, whether we are being conformed to the broken and corrupt pattern of the world, or to the good and whole image of Christ.[172] This, then, is a conscious matter of breathing in the Word and Spirit, before we breathe out in our presence, speech and acts. Together with others, we may intentionally choose to find Jesus, learn from him, put his teaching into practice and let his Spirit conform us to his image in every way.

An excellent contemporary examination of this is *The Disciple* written by Lucy Peppiatt.[173] Lucy is a theologian and president of WTC Theology. She is also a wife, mother to four grown boys, and a grandparent. So her experience – in church, work, ministry, and at home – is normal, recognisable and helpful as she outlines what formation looks like today. Lucy

172. Robert Mulholland: *Invitation to a Journey: A Roadmap for Spiritual Formation* (Menlo Park, CA: IVP, 2016) and *Shaped by the Word* (Nashville, TN: Upper Room Books, 2023).
173. Published: Eugene, OR: Cascade Books, 2012.

points out that we are formed by the Word, the Spirit, life and one another. Each of the sections she covers, as well as the formation that comes through serving and giving, are accompanied by a set of habits, practices, or ways of learning more about the way of Jesus through life experience. The emphasis here is not on a separately compartmented life which is 'spiritual', but instead working out how to be spiritual in our everyday occupation and the way we spend our time. That will include listening out for God's word to us when someone is preaching or teaching or reading the Bible more prayerfully. It could mean becoming more aware of what season we are walking through in life – party, desert, battle, victory – and learning to follow Jesus in new ways accordingly. It may be about the kind of deep, secure and pure friendships we can nurture and develop that both stretch and comfort us in our own pursuit of holiness. Everything in life contributes to, or challenges our following of Jesus. Looking at life and holiness this way means that we are not necessarily adding lots of extra burdens and things-to-do-that-make-us-better-Christians (which was the Pharisees' approach), but instead we fulfil Romans 12:1 by offering our lives as living sacrifices. Doing life, in the Holy Spirit, is the way to live life and enjoy it. Ultimately of course, we are called to give up everything to follow Jesus. There is no greater life! What a risk! But, says Lucy, what a life of courage – countercultural, demanding, but so exciting!

> I have discovered the value of fixing Scripture in my heart by way of memorisation (Psalm 119:9-11; Proverbs 4:23). For a long while, memorising Scripture has been a daily habit, and nowadays I am able to recall many times when a verse or two has come to mind and helped me in an unexpected moment of my life.
>
> (Robin Vincent, Care for the Family)

Becoming disciples together

As mentioned earlier, Cris Rogers has written the book *Making Disciples*. This is a book of exercises that help us think through how we are being formed and able to follow Jesus well. We used an exercise from it in the Playground section of our previous chapter. Cris is a vicar and he loves being part of a church community, so this is written in such a way that it highlights discipleship with one another. His emphasis is on head, heart and hands: how our minds are renewed with the knowledge and awareness of the grace and truth of Jesus; how our characters are changed when our hearts are aligned with Christ in desires, hopes, care and love; how we combine faith and deed – not just believing in and about Jesus – but putting this into practice with actions and behaviours that demonstrate our faith. For Cris, these aspects of who we are, are best developed within a community which has developed a culture of discipleship-making informed by their beliefs, values and practices. It is impossible to learn how to be a disciple of Jesus from a textbook – just like learning to drive cannot be done without actually getting in a car and daring to use the clutch. Cris says himself that he cannot just be told what to do to follow Jesus, he needs to be developed and shown ways how to do this. Cris' handbook, then, is for groups of people to use, and talk, pray and act together in such a way that they help

> My wife and I run two microchurches, both of which have non-Christian friends and neighbours. We study the Scriptures together and pray, encouraging them within those moments (and in separate chats) to keep journeying with us – and Jesus.
>
> (Matt Summerfield, Zeo Church, Hitchin, Reboot Your Leadership)

form one another. Who can you do this with? Perhaps agree with some friends or in a group at church that you will use this book or a similar tool to grow together as followers of Jesus. And then see how that impacts your personal lives as well as what you do together to obey Jesus.

Committing to each other for the sake of following Jesus

A good example of a wholehearted follower of Jesus is John Wesley. He was especially concerned about how to grow and sustain faith beyond the moments of inspirational teaching and worship in larger settings. His concern, learned from the parable of the sower, was that if the seed did not find good soil then the new life would quickly be choked, dried up or snatched away. His challenge was to develop good soil in a believer's heart. He learned from others about smaller, accountable groups where individuals would share their life of faith with one another. One example of this happening was among the Moravian community in Germany. They were prayerful, mission orientated and committed to social engagement. They also prioritised teaching. But what impressed Wesley were the small bands that met once or twice a week to confess sins and pray. Inspired by this, he went on to start class meetings where members would meet weekly, sing a hymn, and then share the progress and challenges of their spiritual lives. They were carrying each other's burdens, loving each other, and becoming closer to Jesus. They took one another seriously and gave and accepted correction and discipline. They also contributed financially to give to the poor. The fruit of the spirit that grows from this way of mutual discipleship then displays itself and enriches the world around with the same gospel. This became the basis for the phenomenon that became the Methodist movement across the world.

Do you have friendships that give this kind of room for worship and discipleship; where honesty and mutual encouragement fulfil Scripture of confessing sins, bringing restoration, sharing burdens and doing good for one another? Wesley found that

> I have a video app on my phone that enables me to connect regularly with my most trusted friend/mentor who lives across the world. Whatever I am experiencing, be it parenting issues, church leadership complexity, or questions about faith, culture or managing stress, she gives advice, prays, challenges and shares her own experience. I find myself referring back to her advice very regularly. More than that, I intentionally make space to be there for others in a similar way. After all, if you have experienced a blessing, you want to share it and to replicate what you have been blessed with.
>
> Living for Jesus can look like a lot of things. For us, it has also involved learning to follow Jesus as we live with disability within our marriage. Mark's sight loss has meant huge adjustments for him, but also for me as his wife. Each day, Mark chooses to follow Jesus despite his limitations, and each day I ask for God's help in supporting, serving, assisting, driving or showing compassion when it is hard for him. This isn't always easy, but I am constantly brought back to how Jesus showed such care for those with physical and emotional needs, stopping, slowing down, caring and meeting their needs in the way only he could. For us, we rely on him for patience and perseverance and we trust he will use us despite our limits or frustrations. We have learned that when we are weak, his strength never fails.
>
> (Cathy Madavan, Speaker and Author)

these groups, which were so 'up' and 'in' focused were actually the very reason why people wanted to come to faith in Jesus. Lives lived in obedience to Jesus are attractive! It is a great way of living. Who doesn't want love, security, forgiveness, power, friendship and direct access to the maker of the universe? Wesley preached to crowds but it was the living witness of these small bands of followers that made the connection and demonstrated the glory of being a Christian to those around.

On the road: A story

In the Bible study section of this chapter, we will be looking at Bartimaeus, who was by the side of the road when Jesus met him, but who jumped up, left his cloak, and followed Jesus after a very special encounter. I have had a number of crossroad moments in my life, where I have chosen to put faith into practice and follow Jesus on the road even though it meant leaving behind even what had been good and helpful. Bev and I were really enjoying leading a congregation of a larger network of churches in London. We had wonderful friends with whom we also enjoyed serving Jesus. There were plenty of amazing Christian leaders around us, many of whom are well-known friends of Spring Harvest, doing imaginative and fruitful exploits for God. And we felt God say to leave it all behind and go to another town and another church. It was hard because these were our dear friends. There was also a challenge from the Holy Spirit (via an annoyingly helpful person): could we follow Jesus without being surrounded by all this gifting, skill and passion? Could we trust in God and his resource rather than perhaps rely on other people's faith and work? Moving – following Jesus on a new road – was not easy. I don't think I jumped up like Bartimaeus; rather I reluctantly shuffled up to the Midlands.

A few years later, after lots of hard work and the forming of new friendships, it felt that it may be time to move on. Things were good but I was missing some of the dynamism of what I had previously experienced. I didn't think I could imagine it fully being expressed where I was, unless there was some fundamental change. I wanted more, for me and the church – but felt that it was stuck. After looking wherever I could for an easy way out, I eventually felt challenged by Jesus that I had to be courageous. This was not the time to leave but the time to stand up, declare a vision and a dream, and see who wanted to join in. Standing up can feel intimidating. What if people don't like what you say, or don't want to go in that direction? What if people you respect don't agree with you? What if you have to leave with your tail between your legs because your ideas don't really fit with the family you are a part of? I felt all that, but eventually described to the church what kind of church we could be – living for others, less defensive, passionate for the presence of God, and eager to live out our faith in our everyday lives and not just within church. I wondered if everyone would rather not stretch out like this but would like to remain as they were – which is often the case in church life, actually. But in fact, everyone wanted it! We even voted for it! And that year so much changed; so many mission initiatives took off; worship and prayer became more passionate; welcome became a watchword, and the church grew.

And more recently, another following Jesus on the road episode. I have loved working in the church – all the dimensions of up, in and out. But about four years ago, felt yet another annoying stirring of challenge for courageous living once more. This time it was to step out from the relative security of church leadership, and learn to live more fully by faith; to follow the Holy Spirit and trust in him for guidance, purpose and provision. After lots of consideration and asking for advice, it felt the right step – in fact, plenty of people said it was obvious and I should just get on with it and stop procrastinating. But for me it was another jumping-up-and-leaving-the-former-things-behind moment. And now it is this on a daily basis. Can I follow without all those resources and a team around me? Can I follow when I'm no longer a church leader, and paid to be a good Christian? Can I follow when there isn't a defined role? Can I follow when I don't know where the money is coming from? Can I follow when it is dependent on the faint whisper of the Spirit? Can I follow not just when the prayers are being answered but when I'm still waiting in faith for what I believe God has promised?

Artist: Helen Yousaf

Playground

For all the resources, links and information about the contributors mentioned, scan the code to visit:

www.springharvest.org/resources/no-greater-life/

Practices

Which disciplines explored through this journey have most helped you? Put one or two into practice now.

John Wesley used questions to ask one another to encourage accountability. Find some people to use these questions with.

https://www.umc.org/en/content/john-wesleys-22-questions-of-self-examination

For a selection of more questions also found in *Cultivating a Life for Good* by Neil Cole (St Charles, IL: ChurchSmart Resources, 1999).

https://ctkbraselton.org/wp-content/uploads/2021/09/Small-Group-Accountability-Questions.pdf

Resources

Bible Society have plenty of resources, including the excellent 'The Bible Course', for learning from and allowing the Bible to challenge and change our hearts as disciples. www.biblesociety.org.uk/resources

Christianity Explored also have a number of courses as well as their well-known course for those interested in faith. For instance, their discipleship course based on the book of Philippians. www.christianityexplored.org/courses/discipleship-explored/

Lectio Divina 5

Harvest Time
Luke 9:57 – 10:2

As we draw this journey to a close, let's pause and pray with a *Lectio 365* Morning Prayer, meditating on the cost of following Jesus.

Together we will pray (P.R.A.Y.): P – pausing to be still, R – rejoicing with a psalm and reflecting on Scripture, A – asking God to help us and others and Y – yielding to his will in our lives.

Pause

As I enter prayer now, I pause to be still; to breathe slowly; to re-centre my scattered senses upon the presence of God.

Pause and pray

Prayer of Approach

Jesus, light of the world,
As I follow you today would you illuminate the darkness within me and around me.
Show me your presence and your path as I welcome the light of life.

(Adapted from John 8:12)

Rejoice and reflect

I choose to rejoice in God's majesty today, joining with the ancient praise of all God's people in the words of Psalm 46:

'Be still, and know that I am God!
I will be honored by every nation.
I will be honored throughout the world.'
The Lord of Heaven's Armies is here among us;
the God of Israel is our fortress.

(Psalm 46:10-11, NLT)

Pause and pray

Jesus and his disciples are travelling through Samaria. Jesus is resolutely making his way to Jerusalem for the completion of his mission. Every moment counts as the day of his death approaches . . .

As they were walking along the road, a man said to him, 'I will follow you wherever you go.'
Jesus replied, 'Foxes have dens and birds have nests, but the Son of Man has nowhere to lay his head.'
He said to another man, 'Follow me.'
But he replied, 'Lord, first let me go and bury my father.'
Jesus said to him, 'Let the dead bury their own dead, but you go and proclaim the kingdom of God.'
Still another said, 'I will follow you, Lord; but first let me go back and say goodbye to my family.'
Jesus replied, 'No one who puts a hand to the plough and looks back is fit for service in the kingdom of God.'
After this the Lord appointed seventy-two others and sent them two by two ahead of him to every town and place where he was about to go. He told them, 'The harvest is plentiful, but the workers are few. Ask the Lord of the harvest, therefore, to send out workers into his harvest field.

(Luke 9:57 – 10:2)

As I reflect on this passage I notice three types of followers. First, there is the hasty and idealistic one, eager to jump in and follow Jesus without counting the cost. Second, there is the procrastinating disciple, who wants to follow Jesus later . . . sometime. And third, there is the indecisive disciple, torn between two allegiances. But Jesus' response to each is full of urgency. This is not the moment for half measures or delay. 'The harvest is plentiful' – am I ready to get to work?

Ask

Where do I find myself in this passage? Which disciple do I relate to the most?

Forgive me, Lord, for those times I am too quick, too slow or too undecided. I bring you the worries or obstacles that are holding me back . . .

Pause and pray

God, I pray for the missionaries in my town and the people I know across the world who have counted the cost and are following You into the mission field. Strengthen them today when the cost feels very big.

Pause and pray

Yield

As I return to today's passage, I explore it with my imagination. I imagine myself among the disciples listening in on Jesus' conversation. What do I see, hear, smell, taste or sense in this story?

> As they were walking along the road, a man said to him, 'I will follow you wherever you go.'
> Jesus replied, 'Foxes have dens and birds have nests, but the Son of Man has nowhere to lay his head.'
> He said to another man, 'Follow me.'
> But he replied, 'Lord, first let me go and bury my father.'

> Jesus said to him, 'Let the dead bury their own dead, but you go and proclaim the kingdom of God.'
> Still another said, 'I will follow you, Lord; but first let me go back and say goodbye to my family.'
> Jesus replied, 'No one who puts a hand to the plough and looks back is fit for service in the kingdom of God.'
> After this the Lord appointed seventy-two others and sent them two by two ahead of him to every town and place where he was about to go. He told them, 'The harvest is plentiful, but the workers are few. Ask the Lord of the harvest, therefore, to send out workers into his harvest field.
>
> (Luke 9:57 – 10:2)

I continue to linger in this passage, allowing the scene to come to life in my imagination . . .

Pause

I am struck by the image of the plough. Ploughing in ancient times was hard work that required focus and concentration. To plough in a straight line, I would have had to look to the far end of the field, pick one visual destination, and then not turn my eyes until I reached my destination. Looking back would mean spoiling the work. Jesus invites me to give him my unwavering focus.

Pause and pray

Prayer of Yielding

Jesus, it's easy to leave church on Sunday, ready to give you my all, but by Wednesday my passion has sometimes cooled and the demands and worries of life have diverted my focus. What would it mean to fix my eyes firmly on you this week? What practice or reminder would I need to help me stay the course?

Yielding Promise

And now, as I prepare to take this time of prayer into the coming day, the Lord who loves me says in Hebrews:

> Therefore, since we are surrounded by such a great cloud of witnesses, let us throw off everything that hinders and the sin that so easily entangles. And let us run with perseverance the race marked out for us, fixing our eyes on Jesus, the pioneer and perfecter of faith . . . Consider him who endured . . . so that you will not grow weary and lose heart.
>
> (Hebrews 12:1-3)

Closing prayer

Father, help me to live this day to the full,
being true to you, in every way.
Jesus, help me to give myself away to others,
being kind to everyone I meet.
Spirit, help me to love the lost,
proclaiming Christ in all I do and say.

Amen

Lectio 365 is a prayer app from 24-7 Prayer. Download for free to pray the Bible morning, noon and night.

Deuteronomy 30:15-20; Deuteronomy 31:7-8; Colossians 1:9-14 (ESV)

 Journal – pray, reflect, write

Refer to: For the Journey: www.bible.com/reading-plans/14926-journey-to-know-god-find-freedom-discover-purpose

Make notes of your own journey from finding faith/what led you to make a decision to be a disciple, through the key challenges, growth times, disappointments and breakthroughs.

....

....

....

....

As you look at this map of your own journey, what is Jesus saying to you about his and your own faithfulness?

....

....

....

....

Who has helped you on this journey? Who have you helped?

....

....

....

....

In what ways have you had the strength and humility of the women in Mark's Gospel, and where do you need to put that into practice at the moment?

....

....

....

....

Worship/Prayer

Read Psalm 107 as a prayer. If possible, do this with some others with whom you are on the journey of faith. Ask one another which verses most resonate, and pray for each other.

Action

Moses called the people together to remember, celebrate and plan for their future. When was the last time you did this in your church or among friends? Plan an event where your own stories of faith and following can be told, and new covenants made. It could be with just a few close Christian friends, or with a much larger group.

Jesus pretty much insisted that this should include food, and that we remember him at the heart of it. Plan a great menu of food and drink you all love.

Eat, pray, celebrate.

Group Bible study

A tale of two journeys: choose life

Mark 10:17-27 and Mark 10:46-52

- Jesus is on an important journey in both stories. What is his response to being interrupted?
- The man who has followed the law seems genuine and committed. Following commands is what we have seen to be encouraged in Deuteronomy, so what is right and wrong about his heart? In what ways might following the rules obscure who Jesus is?
- Bartimaeus is physically blind but spiritually open – he knows Jesus as the Son of David. What does this mean?
- The man runs up to Jesus, falls to his knees and calls him teacher. What does this say about him? Are we that keen?
- Bartimaeus is rebuked but carries on shouting then threw away his cloak (his means of security) and leapt up. What does this say about him? Are we that keen?
- The young man does not follow but goes away, on his own, sad. Bartimaeus is healed and follows Jesus with the others on the road. Talk together about this, how you feel and how Jesus felt.
- Who in these stories are you like, and why or why not?

Wholehearted – a series of studies about the heart #5

Stephen and Mara, who were mentioned earlier in their work on Heartstyles, counted the number of times that the word heart or hearts is written in the King James Version of the Bible. It is 911 times! That is more than fear, fears and afraid; more than good and goodness, more than sin, more even than love, more than faith and more than hope. Here is a selection of Bible verses about the heart that we have not yet covered in this book.

> Blessed are those whose strength is in you, whose hearts are set on pilgrimage.
>
> (Psalm 84:5)

> But I trust in your unfailing love; my heart rejoices in your salvation.
>
> (Psalm 13:5)

> These people honour me with their lips, but their hearts are far from me.
>
> (Matthew 15:8)

> Above all else, guard your heart, for everything you do flows from it.
>
> (Proverbs 4:23)

Anxiety weighs down the heart, but a kind word cheers it up.

(Proverbs 12:25)

A cheerful heart is good medicine, but a crushed spirit dries up the bones.

(Proverbs 17:22)

For as he thinks in his heart, so is he.

(Proverbs 23:7, NKJV)

Let us draw near to God with a sincere heart and with the full assurance that faith brings, having our hearts sprinkled to cleanse us from a guilty conscience and having our bodies washed with pure water.

(Hebrews 10:22)

The goal of this command is love, which comes from a pure heart and a good conscience and a sincere faith.

(1 Timothy 1:5)

My goal is that they may be encouraged in heart and united in love . . .

(Colossians 2:2)

Now that you have purified yourselves by obeying the truth so that you have sincere love for each other, love one another deeply, from the heart.

(1 Peter 1:22)

Read out these verses and reflect on each of them together.

Questions

How is God speaking to you through them?

Are there other verses about the heart in the rest of this book that have struck you?

How can you read the Bible differently so that the Holy Spirit speaks to your heart through Scripture in such a way that you can be convicted, surprised, enlightened and strengthened to live wholeheartedly?

Pray for one another's hearts, to love God, one another and the world and live for Jesus.

Conclusion: What's Next for Us?

There's no greater life than that lived by Jesus. Jesus truly loved God with all his heart, soul, mind and strength; and loved all his neighbours like himself, as well as his close friends, and even those who were against him and killed him. He is the ultimate disciple in Mark's Gospel. He is also the 'spiritual rock' that accompanied Moses and the Israelites, and from whom they all drank as they journeyed in the wilderness (1 Corinthians 10:4).

Jesus lived every day fully devoted. Because of this, he made sure that all he was about was soaked in his love for God and others. He had a plan, a strategy, and he knew where to go, how to get there and why. But on this journey, he was able to fulfil the Great Commandment at every turn, even when interrupted or in the face of opposition and disappointment. A great story of his three-dimensional life – one of only a very few that is covered by all four Gospel writers – is the feeding of the 5,000. This is probably a good one to finish with because it reminds us of Moses and his teaching too, and is an example of living with eyes fixed on heaven and also living fully, fruitfully and joyfully on the earth. We see in this story all three dimensions of upward, inward and outward wholehearted love.

Up: All the people come to Jesus and find him in a 'solitary place' (Mark 6:32,35). He is modelling a strategic spiritual withdrawal away from the busyness of world where he can be with his heavenly Father. Ironically, everyone joins him and interrupts him, but he invites them to join in with his feeding on the Word of God. Then we see clearly the direction of his heart: '. . . looking up to heaven, he gave thanks . . .' (vv. 34,41)

In: His disciples deliberately come to him (a word that Mark uses when people approach Jesus for a confrontation) to complain, in verses 35 and 36. But Jesus includes them in what he is about to do. Despite their negativity he leads them as a team and gets them working well with him and one another in looking for some food, so he and they can do something miraculous together, in verses 37 and 38. He continues to work with them by blessing the bread and breaking it. Then he literally 'kept giving' it to them to hand out in verse 41. This is the big supper before the last supper. This is Moses in the wilderness and the manna from heaven. This is God himself providing; doing it in and through community so everyone can be included in learning and growing.

Out: Jesus sees the large crowd and has compassion on them because they are 'like sheep without a shepherd' (v. 34). We see his heart for people and it is this big heart of love that motivates him to not only teach them ('many things', Mark says!), but also to give them all a free lunch. He organises them so that they can have the best experience and enjoy eating together in community in verses 39 and 40. He then gives them so much food that everyone is fully 'satisfied' and there is lots left over – symbolically, enough for everyone who was not there, too! (vv. 42-43).

This is a great way of living life. This is literally heaven on earth. The God of Israel doing his manna feeding again, but this time on green grass, sitting in groups, overcoming arguments and being close enough to touch. It takes prayer, blessing, compassion, faith, friends and generosity. And five loaves and two fish.

This is the journey of our hearts:

To pray and to bless
To make a home and welcome others in
To go, to send, to serve and to speak
To love God with all our hearts, soul, mind and strength
and love our neighbour as ourselves.

Final Top Tips on Discipleship

Learn to turn those 'what ifs' of fear (what if I fail?) into 'even ifs' of faith (even if I fail, he won't fail me). That means trusting God with what we can't control (most things in life!) and being obedient in the things we can control (our own actions, attitudes, thoughts etc). It's how we learn to lean not on our own understanding and resources, but in all our ways and on all our roads in life, we increasingly learn to lean on him.

(Arianna Walker, Mercy Ministries)

So my top tip is to catch any false beliefs, challenge them, and change them to line up with the kingdom of heaven – and then your lifestyle will line up too, allowing you to better serve God and others and be fit for more of what he has for you.

(Gaynor van der Burton, FitFish)

My top tip for being a disciple on the road with Jesus is to find at least three deep, mutual, spiritual friendships. Just like Cleopas and his mate on their way to Emmaus, the Lord often appears as a third presence when friends are together (Luke 24:31-32). When I walk, talk and pray with my friends, the Great Commandment somehow takes care of itself, because in that moment I'm not only moved to love God more but the vulnerability of prayer draws me closer to my friend and spurs me to love my neighbour. These kinds of friendships aren't born overnight but are formed by regularly meeting up and slowly disclosing more of ourselves with each other.

(Sheridan Voysey, Speaker, Broadcaster, Author, Friendship Lab)

Daily wonder and daily surrender.

(Matt Summerfield, Zeo Church, Hitchin, Reboot Your Leadership)

Look around and be distressed; look within and be depressed; look to Jesus and be at rest. Stay humble.

(Simon Guillebaud, Speaker and Author, Great Lakes Outreach, Burundi)

To remain steadfast in faith, to love others, and to become all things to all people, so that some may be saved.

(John O'Connor, Junction 42)

To be a disciple of Jesus we must not simply love him and be loved but we must also action this love into obeying what he teaches us to do. We must not see discipleship as simply our spiritual formation but also as our daily spiritual activity in the world. Faith and action.

(Cris Rogers, Spring Harvest, All Hallows Church Bow, Making Disciples)

A little while ago I was having a hard time. I sat to pray with a friend and had a really powerful image of Jesus on a small sail boat with me. He wasn't steering the ship or standing on the hull giving a sermon. He was sitting beside me, chatting; passing the time, on the journey. I've never let go of that powerful image of Jesus and whenever I feel overwhelmed I say to myself, 'It's you and me, Jesus, and that's all that matters.' It gives me such peace and relief from the trap of people pleasing or fitting in with culture.

(Philippa Hanna, Singer Songwriter)

The best tip I can give anyone on the road following Jesus is this – be faithful in the small things that are in front of you right now. Things done for the sake of Jesus' love are never small in His eyes – even washing the dishes!

(Susanne Willdig, Open Ears: Speech to Text)

Walk in the Rabbi's dust, recognise truly being discipled can be messy, but God brings order to mess if you are really truly have the desire to be shaped by him and friends.

(Dan Hargreaves, Alive Church Lincoln)

Living a life that relates to Deuteronomy 24 – leave a margin around the edge of your life – around your field, around your orchard and around your vineyard. You've got to leave a margin for others to taste the fruit of your fields – living out of the overflow so people experience the best of you.

(Tania Bright, Safe Families/Home for Good)

Show up. Consistently. Humbly. Prayerfully.
You don't need to have it all together – just be willing.
As ROC often says, ordinary people can do extraordinary things when they step out in love. Whether you're handing out flip-flops, mentoring a child, or offering a quiet conversation – Jesus is in it.

(Debra Green, Redeeming Our Communities)

Pray, Read and Church. Keep it honest, keep it simple, keep it going.

(Nicky Wong, All Hallows Church, Bow)

We are so precious to God that He died to give us life – we need to own this truth, walk in it joyfully, and help others know the same.

(Alexandra Huggins, Faith in Later Life)

People, and relationships, all work differently but for me I keep my best discipline with routine – having regular, planned times to reflect on and with God – this allows me to be more aware of, and engage with, the more spontaneous opportunities that also arise.

(Peter Wilson, Spring Harvest, Physiotherapist)

My top tip . . . live each day like it matters the most.

(Leon Evans, Lifecentral Church, Further Faster Network)

Keeping my eyes firmly fixed on Jesus, and letting him lead me, his way not mine.

(Rosie Giles, Spring Harvest)

Whatever you do to follow . . . Keep it simple, keep it honest and keep it going. And above everything else, and despite everything or anything that happens, try to remember the wisdom of Proverbs 3:5-8. I have often said it this way – the God of the curve will make your path straight.

(Robin Vincent, Care for the Family)

Try to remember you are a disciple of Jesus, not the other way round.

(Rob Parsons, Care for the Family)

Dare to pray 'Lord have your way' and then having the courage following the way he leads.

(Damian Wharton, Scripture Union Northern Ireland)

We are not called to walk alone, so don't. Find your Aaron and Hur – brothers/sisters who will hold your arms up when you're weary, people who will encourage you and spur you on – and be that for someone else. 'A friend hears the song in my heart and sings it back to me when my memory fails' (Unknown).

(Warren Evans, Sports Chaplaincy UK)

Catch, challenge, and change your thoughts. Our lifestyle flows from our habits, which flow from our actions, which are driven by our thoughts. The health of our thought life is a powerful place to start. As believers, we have the advantage of knowing the Truth, and when we align our beliefs with it, our whole life begins to line up too. That's how we become fit for more of what He has for us.

(Gaynor van der Burton, FitFish)

Go a bit slower and with others. Zoom out from time to time, to allow a bigger picture to help us see things we are missing and serve locally more effectively.

(Alan Charter, Children Everywhere Walking With Jesus)

Artist: Debs Last

Acknowledgements

This book is inspired by the team at Spring Harvest and the wider group of friends, ministries, partners and contributors for its Easter Event and year-round work: in particular, Abby Guinness, who was Head of Spring Harvest and her successor, Jo Moir, along with Cris Rogers and the Event Planning Group which is managed by Alice O'Kane. The wisdom, experience and passionately lived out discipleship from all the various contributors to this book – each of whom has played a significant part in the Spring Harvest event – is very much appreciated.

With special thanks to Carla Harding who has generously provided material from 24-7 Prayer's Lectio 365. The spirit of unity, friendship and co-working for the sake of the Kingdom of God is a beautiful reflection of wholehearted discipleship.

Thank you too for all the input from Malcolm, Sarah Grace, Sheila and Lydia at Malcolm Down Publishers.

The *No Greater Life* Leader's Toolkit

Bring the transformative teaching of this book to your church or small group with our comprehensive digital toolkit.

Designed for leaders who want to go deeper, this creative resource pack provides everything you need to facilitate a life-changing discipleship experience:

- **Creative Sermon Outlines:** Fresh, engaging frameworks built on solid biblical foundations.
- **Small Group Studies:** Further thoughtful notes to help your community explore *No Greater Life* together.
- **Exclusive Bulk Discounts:** Special pricing is available for churches and groups ordering multiple copies.

Find out more at
www.malcolmdown.co.uk/no-greater-life-toolkit

Experience *No Greater Life* On The Go

E-Book: Perfect for highlighting and searching key insights.

Audiobook: Let the teaching come alive through your headphones.

Search for *No Greater Life* on your favourite digital bookstore or audiobook provider today.

www.ingramcontent.com/pod-product-compliance
Lightning Source LLC
LaVergne TN
LVHW020041110826
845155LV00029B/575

* 9 7 8 1 9 1 7 4 5 5 5 1 0 *